Contents

Indian red-liveried Furness Railway No. 3 'Coppernob', seen on display in the Great Hall at the National Railway Museum in York in January 2017, has been preserved since it was withdrawn from traffic in 1900. Its nickname derives from the copper cladding to its dome-shaped 'haystack' firebox. Built in 1846 by Bury, Curtis, and Kennedy of Liverpool, it is an 0-4-0 version of Edward Bury's popular bar-frame design of the period, with iron bar frames and inside cylinders. It is the only survivor of this type in Britain. Ending its working life on shunting duties around Barrow-in-Furness docks, it was preserved in a glass pavilion at Barrow station, and has shrapnel wounds following a Luftwaffe attack during the Second World War. ROBIN JONES

GREAT BRITISH STEAM
The National Collection

COVER MAIN PICTURE: LMS Pacific No. 6229 *Duchess of Hamilton* and LNER A4 4-6-2 No. 4468 *Mallard* in the Great Hall of the National Railway Museum. BRIAN SHARPE

COVER INSETS: LNER A3 Pacific No. 60103 *Flying Scotsman* climbs towards Ais Gill at Mallerstang with a Railway Touring Company 'Waverley' tour from York to Carlisle on July 16, 2017. JOHN DUNGATE

Bulleid Pacific No. 34051 *Winston Churchill* at the NRM. ROBIN JONES

C000129625

EDITOR:
Robin Jones
rjones@mortons.co.uk

PRODUCTION EDITOR:
Sarah Palmer

DESIGNER:
Craig Lamb
design_lamb@btinternet.com

COVER DESIGN:
Michael Baumber

REPROGRAPHICS:
Paul Fincham and Jonathan Schofield

ADVERTISING:
Craig Amess
camess@mortons.co.uk

PUBLISHERS:
Steve O'Hara, Tim Hartley

PUBLISHING DIRECTOR:
Dan Savage

COMMERCIAL DIRECTOR:
Nigel Hole

MARKETING MANAGER:
Charlotte Park
cpark@mortons.co.uk

PRINTED BY:
William Gibbons and Sons, Wolverhampton

ISBN:
978-1-911276-41-8

PUBLISHED BY:
Mortons Media Group Ltd, Media Centre, Morton Way, Horncastle, Lincolnshire LN9 6JR. Tel: 01507 529529

MORTONS
MEDIA GROUP LTD

Saving steel-wheeled treasures for the nation

Britain's National Railway Museum is far and away the finest of its kind in the world.

Indeed, nothing less would suffice for the nation that invented and honed to perfection the steam locomotive and started the railway revolution, which in the wake of the Industrial Revolution, shrank the globe.

For first-time visitors to the York museum, venturing inside its doors is like walking straight into the pages of a glossy Hornby model train catalogue. There in front of you are locomotives big and small that changed the course of transport

history and became living legends.

In Britain, we are gifted with a National Collection of historic railway vehicles, not just steam locomotives but diesels and electrics, plus a plethora of carriages and wagons.

However, the road to preserving these icons has been far from easy, and so many treasures of similar magnitude were lost to the scrapman before the powers that be acknowledged either their historical worth or their mass public appeal.

The first locomotive to be preserved anywhere in the world was *Invicta*, built by Robert Stephenson & Co in Newcastle in

1829, immediately after *Rocket* was supplied to the Canterbury & Whitstable Railway, hauling its inaugural train on May 3, 1830.

Retired in 1836 as the railway took a retrograde step and switched to cable haulage by stationary engines, *Invicta* was set aside in 1839.

It came into the ownership of the South Eastern Railway and was exhibited at the golden jubilee of the Stockton & Darlington Railway in 1875 and at the Newcastle Stephenson Centenary in 1881.

For decades kept as a curio in a

North Eastern Railway 2-2-4T No. 66 *Aerolite* was built in 1869 as a replacement for an engine of the same name built by Kitson for the Great Exhibition in 1851, which was destroyed in a collision in 1868. The engine, like its predecessor, was used to haul the mechanical engineer's saloon. Originally a 2-2-2WT well tank, side tanks were added 1886, and around this time it received the number 66. In 1892 *Aerolite* was rebuilt into a 4-2-2, destroying much of the original engine, but 1902 it was again rebuilt into a 2-2-4T.

Being completely non-standard and with a unique wheel arrangement, it was classified X1 by the LNER, but continued in service doing the job it was originally designed for until it was withdrawn in 1933 and preserved in 1934 at the LNER's York museum. It is now a static exhibit at the NRM in York but because of its many changes, it is not considered representative of any particular design era or type. ROBIN JONES

South Eastern & Chatham Railway 1901-built Wainwright D 4-4-0 No. 737, the sole survivor of a class of 51, was earmarked for preservation by the British Transport Commission in 1953 and when withdrawn three years later, was placed in store at Tweedmouth. In 1959 it was restored at Ashford Works and eventually handed over to the National Railway Museum, where it is now on display in the Great Hall.

Lancashire & Yorkshire Railway Chief Mechanical Engineer John Aspinall's Class 5 2-4-2Ts, otherwise known as 'Lanky tanks', replaced 0-4-4Ts, which he considered unbalanced, and had insufficient water capacity. Eventually, 330 2-4-2Ts were built, and they were capable of handling all but the heaviest expresses. The first of the class, No. 1008 is preserved as a static exhibit in the National Railway Museum at York. ROBIN JONES

public park, painted bright red, it is now displayed in Canterbury Heritage Museum in Stour Street.

Of today's survivors, the next to be retained would be the pioneer from the Stockton & Darlington, Locomotion No. 1, which was preserved in 1857.

In 1862, Stephenson's *Rocket* was donated to the Patent Office Museum in London (now the Science Museum) in a much-modified form compared with when it was built for the 1829 Rainhill Trials.

Sadly, Richard Trevithick's 1804 locomotive – which gave the first public

demonstration of a steam railway engine, a watershed moment in the evolution of world technology – did not make it. After years of use as a stationary boiler, it ended up among a pile of scrap purchased by the LNWR. It is said to have been sidelined for short time with preservation in mind, until locomotive superintendent Francis William Webb had a change of heart, and it went to the blast furnace of the LNWR's own steelworks. Several Victorians who savoured the rich fruits of the railway age were astute in saving landmark locomotives after their service days were

over. However, there were others who did not care one bit about history.

Such a man was William Stanier, who designed some of the finest locomotives in the world, including the Princess Royal and Princess Coronation Pacifics, as Chief Mechanical Engineer of the LMS.

The Great Western Railway kept two broad gauge locomotives for posterity; *North Star*, which had been preserved after withdrawal in 1871, and celebrity Iron Duke class 4-2-2 *Lord of the Isles*. Yet while then GWR Chief Mechanical Engineer George Jackson Churchward was away on holiday in 1906, Stanier,

Midland Railway 156 class 2-4-0 No. 158A was one of 29 designed by locomotive superintendent Matthew Kirtley and built at Derby between 1866 and 1874. The LMS recognised the significance of the class and class doyen No. 156 was earmarked for preservation but the decision was overturned and the engine was scrapped in 1932. However, 15 years later, surviving classmate No. 20002 was set aside at Derby after being withdrawn from its last duties as a station pilot at Nottingham.

Despite having been reboilered twice, its front end being much rebuilt, and having a new tender, it was restored to Midland Railway condition as No. 158A. It appeared at the Stephenson Centenary celebrations in Chesterfield in 1948 and was a static exhibit in Birmingham during the centenary celebrations for New Street station in 1954. March 17, 1965 saw it transferred to the National Collection store in the old Midland shed at Hellifield but it was quickly moved to the Midland shed at Leicester in August 1967 and displayed in a small short-lived museum in the city the following year.

It was stored at Derby Locomotive Works until moving to the Midland Railway-Butterley in 1975. It now takes pride of place in the Matthew Kirtley Exhibition Hall at Swanwick Junction. TONY HISGETT*

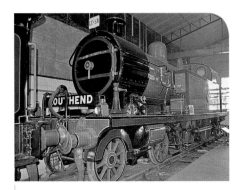

London, Tilbury & Southend Railway 4-4-2T No. 80, built in 1909 for heavy commuter trains, was withdrawn from traffic in 1956 and preserved. It was restored that year by Norwich shedmaster, Bill Harvey, assisted by members of the Norfolk Railway Society to celebrate the centenary of the LTSR, when a special train was run from Southend to London with a restored LTSR carriage in which members of local operatic and dramatic societies travelled in period costume. Thundersley is now on display inside Bressingham Steam Museum.
ASHLEY DACE*

"replaceable relics and archives" which were now part of its remit.

Following a series of representations, BTC chairman Sir Cyril Hurcombe (later Lord Hurcourt) agreed that a list should be drawn up of locomotives worth saving for historical reasons.

However, at a 1948 meeting on the subject, the Railway Executive's mechanical engineer Robert Riddles, who oversaw the development of the British Railways Standard classes, argued that locomotives should be preserved only in exceptional circumstances and that in other cases, scale models would suffice.

A committee was set up within the BTC to consider steps to preserve railway "relics" and records and in 1951 published a report emphasising the importance of not only preserving items already withdrawn from traffic, but also earmarking those still in use. Its key recommendations were that the BTC should continue the policy of the Big Four in identifying engines and coaches for preservation, and a new national transport museum in London, perhaps at the former LSWR depot and sheds at Nine Elms, with smaller regional collections in Edinburgh and Cardiff.

The report, perhaps most importantly, called for the creation of the new posts of a curator of relics and an archivist. This is held to be the beginnings of what we now know as the National Collection.

John Scholes became the curator of relics with LC Johnson, former registrar of the LMS, archivist.

In 1956 the BTC published Transport Treasures, a booklet written by Talyllyn Railway saviour Tom Rolt which listed the 42 locomotives, 35 items of railway rolling stock, and five tramcars then preserved, and referred to the proposed national transport museum. A former London Transport tram and later bus depot at Clapham in south London was chosen as the site for a national museum of transport. In 1961, it was opened as the British Transport Museum.

A POLICY FOR AN ARBITRARY COLLECTION?
In 1957, Stratford Works destroyed several vehicles earmarked for preservation, notably a Great Eastern Railway tram engine and a coach from the Wisbech & Upwell Tramway.

The wave of anger that followed led the following year to then BTC chairman Sir Brian Robertson setting up the Consultative Panel for the Preservation of British Transport Relics with the remit to recommend items that should be saved. Broadly speaking, the BTC accepted its recommendations, but it has been said that they were inconsistent and reflected panel members' personal preferences and ideas.

The policy was to fill gaps in the existing collection while earmarking examples of the latest and last steam

who was then Swindon Works manager, decided to cut them up to save space, after no museum elsewhere was willing to take them.

Churchward was livid when he returned, and managed to salvage many components of *North Star*, but only the driving wheels from *Lord of the Isles* survived this act of vandalism.

Stanier had no regrets, and after moving to the LMS, ordered four historic locomotives to be cut up in 1932.

A RAILWAY MUSEUM FOR ALL BRITAIN
The concept of a British national railway museum had been proposed and rejected in 1896. However, in 1931, the Commission on Museums and Galleries decided that a catalogue of rolling stock that should be saved for the nation should be compiled, while ruling that a national museum as impractical. Around that time, some redundant locomotives could be seen plinthed in public places.

The day before Nationalisation on January 1, 1948, a letter appeared in The Times calling for the newly formed British Transport Commission to look at engines to run on the national network, as British Railways plunged rapidly into modernisation.

Hindsight is marvellous, but many today question the criteria for saving some locomotives and rejecting others. The most common question asked is why the world's most famous A3 Pacific *Flying Scotsman* was not saved for the nation by the committee, which chose instead to save an A4 as its example of a Gresley Pacific. But for the intervention of Ffestiniog Railway saviour Alan Pegler, No. 4472 would have gone to the scrapyard and the A3 class rendered extinct.

After the BTC folded in 1962, railways were run by the British Railways Board, which had no interest in preservation and in an era typified by the Beeching Axe, pointed out that the museums at Clapham, York and Swindon had lost around £100,000. It recommended the museum be moved from Clapham, the worst of the lossmakers.

In 1963 BR published the Historic Relics Scheme and offered to provide accommodation for a national transport museum in redundant sheds in York. It caused widespread concern among historians and preservationists who felt that some saved items could disappear under an indifferent BR. It was followed by a widespread debate over several years as to whether York was the best choice, with other suggested sites including St Pancras, the former Brighton Works, Peterborough and the Low Level station at Crystal Place.

The Canterbury & Whitstable Railway's Robert Stephenson 0-4-0 *Invicta* was the first locomotive in the world to be preserved, but is not part of the National Collection. It is pictured inside Canterbury Heritage Museum. ROBIN JONES

YORK FIRST AND FOREMOST
In 1972, it was finally decided that the former LNER museum in York would be relocated to a new site in the city and expanded into a national museum.

To cut a long story short, Clapham closed and the National Railway Museum in York opened on September 27, 1975. It was an overnight sensation: within a month of opening, it had recorded

125,000 visitors in one week – and that was in the days before entrance to Britain's national museums was free. It has worked miracles for local tourism over more than four decades, and apart from taking responsibility for the National Collection, has established itself as a centre of excellence for learning about railway history.

Of course, space would always be at a premium, and the museum has always loaned out items from the National Collection, as it became officially known, the other heritage railways and museum venues, as listed in the final chapter in this volume

On October 22, 2004, Prime Minister Tony Blair opened the NRM's new £11.3-million 'outreach' station, Locomotion: The National Railway Museum at Shildon, based on the former Timothy Hackworth Victorian Railway Museum. Locomotion has been a godsend not only in providing much extra display for National Collection stock, but has done much to further the cause of railway heritage in the North East, the "cradle of the railways" in the early days of George Stephenson.

As our railways evolve, there will be more calls for items of everyday traction today to be preserved and therefore will be increasing demands on museum space. That will remain a perpetual challenge to curatorial staff, especially in times such as the post-2008 recession and ensuing years of austerity when budgets for all national museums have been tight.

George Stephenson developed the 'long boiler' design in 1842, in order to keep the centre of gravity of the engine low for increased stability during slower heavier work. Designed by William Bouch using this principle, a total of 192 NER 1001 class long-boiler locomotives were built from 1852 by several private manufacturers, as well as the NER's workshops at Darlington and Shildon. The small size of the firebox would seem remarkable in later years, but the engines were ideal where trains might spend long periods standing, waiting for a path, or when shunting. A minimum amount of fuel would have delivered sufficient heat to the large boiler to start heavy loads.

The last 1001 class was withdrawn in 1923. Having travelled an official mileage of 908,984 miles, No. 1275 was preserved at the LNER's York museum and it is now at the NRM in York. ROBIN JONES

The unique *Gazelle*, believed to be the world's smallest standard gauge steam engine, was built as a 2-2-2 well tank in 1893 by Alfred Dodman & Co of King's Lynn for Norfolk businessman William Burkett who used it for lengthy private excursions both on the Midland & Great Northern Joint Railway and the Great Eastern Railway.

In 1911, it was bought by light railway empire builder Col Holman F Stephens for use as an inspection unit on the Shropshire & Montgomeryshire Railway, where it became the line's No 1, and was later rebuilt as an 0-4-2 well tank for service on that railway's Criggion branch.

During the Second World War, the railway was taken over by the Army and *Gazelle* was used until 1943 when it was withdrawn and preserved. Part of the National Collection, it is now on static display in the Col Stephens Museum at the Kent & East Sussex Railway's Tenterden Town terminus, where it is pictured in 2014. ROBIN JONES

The 1979-built replicas of Stephenson's *Rocket* and two Liverpool & Manchester Railway coaches at Tyseley (Warwick Road) station inside Tyseley Locomotive Works during the June 25, 2011 open weekend. ROBIN JONES

Stephenson's *Rocket* in triplicate
...and a rival twice over

It was not the world's first steam locomotive by any means, but it was the one that steered the future direction of transport technology. The National Collection boasts three versions of Stephenson's *Rocket* – the original, a static replica in the National Railway Museum, and a working version for visits to heritage lines, as well as two versions of *Sans Pareil*, one of its competitors in the legendary Rainhill Trials.

Stephenson's *Rocket* isn't the oldest locomotive in the National Collection, however, in terms of those that went on to become global household names such as *Flying Scotsman* or *Mallard*, it was certainly the first.

Rocket appeared in 1829 – a quarter of a century after Cornish mining engineer Richard Trevithick gave the world's first public demonstration of a steam railway locomotive, on the Penydarren Tramway near Merthyr Tydfil. In those far-off days when life expectancy was so much shorter than today, 25 years was a long time in coming.

Stephenson's *Rocket* was built at the Forth Street Works of Robert Stephenson and Company in Newcastle upon Tyne. Indeed, it has been held to have been

more the work of Robert Stephenson than his father, George, to whom credit for the locomotive is traditionally given.

That year it won the Rainhill Trials held by the Liverpool & Manchester Railway to choose the best design of steam locomotive for the railway, the world's first inter-city line. Indeed, one of the purposes of the trials was to determine, among many other aspects, whether steam locomotives rather than horses were now the premier form of railway traction. Far-off times indeed!

While Trevithick had shown that a self-propelled vehicle was not only feasible but potentially profitable, in 1829 the concept still did not have universal support. By then, only around 50 railway locomotives had been built in England, principally for colliery lines, and the

most powerful of them all was Timothy Hackworth's *Royal George*.

Difficulties with locomotives on both the Hetton and Stockton & Darlington railways were well known, and in the case of the former, one section had been converted to cable haulage, a backward step in the overall scheme of railway history.

Liverpool & Manchester directors remained divided between those, including Stephenson, who favoured locomotives, and those who sided with Stourbridge engineer John Urpeth Rastrick, who argued the case for stationary engines and cable haulage for passenger coaches.

Rastrick incidentally, had not only helped Trevithick with his designs, but in partnership with James Foster, formed

The original *Rocket* in the Science Museum in London, much altered from the condition in which it won the Rainhill Trials. ROBIN JONES

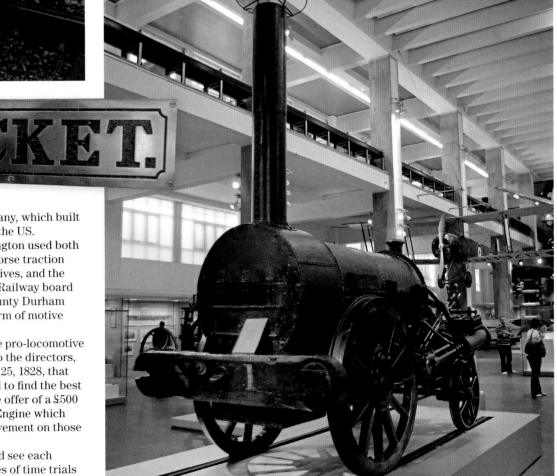

ROCKET.

Foster, Rastrick & Company, which built the *Stourbridge Lion* in the US.

The Stockton & Darlington used both stationary engines and horse traction as well as steam locomotives, and the Liverpool & Manchester Railway board sent observers to the County Durham line to evaluate which form of motive power was the best.

Shortly afterwards the pro-locomotive side presented a report to the directors, they announced on April 25, 1828, that open trials would be held to find the best form of traction, with the offer of a £500 prize for, 'a Locomotive Engine which shall be a decided improvement on those now in use…'

The competition would see each entrant undertake a series of time trials to assess its efficiency.

The Rainhill Trials in full swing, as illustrated in Lives of the Engineers by Samuel Smiles.

THE CONTEST THAT RESHAPED THE WORLD

On August 31, 1829, it was announced that the trials would be held over 1¾ miles at Rainhill on the Liverpool & Manchester, hence the name Rainhill Trials; a defining moment in global transport history.

It was stipulated the entrant locomotives must be capable of covering 70 miles without breaking down. That was the distance of a return trip over the Liverpool & Manchester Railway.

Furthermore, the locomotives were restricted to a weight of 4½ tons on four wheels, which had to be carried on springs to reduce potential damage to the track. Neither could the boiler be too big, in case its weight also led to track damage.

It is believed that George Stephenson began the design of his own entrant, *Rocket*, in May 1829.

He set out to create a machine that was both light in weight yet had a high power rating.

In the contest, it was required to pull a train only three times its own weight, so only the front two wheels needed to be powered.

Completed within a short space of time, the design of *Rocket* – which many historians now believe had a far greater input from Robert Stephenson whereas the credit had been traditionally given to George – brought in several innovations with far-reaching implications beyond Liverpool or Manchester.

The building of *Rocket* began at Robert Stephenson & Co in June and was mostly completed by the end of August.

Rocket underwent its first trials on the Killingworth Railway on September 2 and reached a speed of 8mph up an incline and 12mph on the level.

Further modifications were made before *Rocket* was dismantled and taken by horse-drawn cart from Newcastle

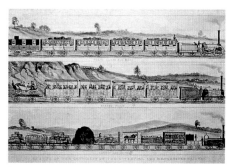

A contemporary sketch of the Rainhill Trials entrants, with *Rocket's* train at the top.

to Carlisle and from there to Liverpool by steamer. It took about two weeks to reassemble *Rocket* so it could undertake further preliminary trials.

The tender was built by Thomas Worsdell at Liverpool and to give the impression of speed and lightness, Rocket was painted in the style of a mail stagecoach.

The paintwork was being touched up not only right until the start of the trials but during them; a young boy riding on the tender became stuck to the cask because the paintwork was still tacky.

A second entrant, *Novelty*, was built in seven weeks in London by John Braithwaite to a design by the Swedish engineer, John Ericsson, but it could not be tested before the trials because there was no railway near London on which it could be run. It was ferried from London to Liverpool by canal boat.

Sans Pareil, which bore similarities to *Royal George*, was built by Hackworth as a private project in his spare time, although the Stockton & Darlington Railway allowed him to use its workshops at Shildon. The 0-4-0 was finished only at the eleventh hour, apart from a run at Aycliffe Level, no prior tests were carried out and it too had a tender built when it arrived in Liverpool just before the big event.

Perseverance, built by Timothy

George Stephenson, who designed *Rocket* with the help of his son, Robert, who built it.

Locomotive engineer, Timothy Hackworth, designed and built *Sans Pareil*, which like its contemporary, *Rocket*, is part of the National Collection.

Timothy Hackworth's *Sans Pareil* was bought by the Liverpool & Manchester Railways after the trials. The remains of the original are housed inside Locomotion: the National Railway Museum at Shildon. ROBIN JONES

LEFT: Scale models of three Rainhill Trials entrants in the National Railway Museum at York. Left to right are *Rocket, Novelty* and *Sans Pareil*. ROBIN JONES

Burstall, was based on a steam road coach design, which he had patented in 1826, and was damaged en route to Rainhill while being unloaded.

Former Liverpool & Manchester director and barrister, Thomas Shaw, who was convinced that steam locomotives were dangerous, entered *Cycloped* - an 'engine' powered by two horses.

Whenever the tethered horses tried to walk or trot, a platform of wooden planks attached to ropes supported by rollers caused two drums to revolve and move the four-wheeled open truck, which comprised the body of the contraption.

Another entrant, Ross Winans, devised a 'manumotive carriage' powered by two men.

To accommodate the trials, George Stephenson was told to prepare a section of double track at Rainhill. The judges included Nicholas Wood, who had ridiculed the idea that locomotives could travel at more than 12mph.

The trials began on Tuesday, October 6 and immediately attracted huge crowds from near and far, including top engineers and scientists of the day.

The first day featured demonstration runs by the competitors, with *Rocket* achieving 18mph while running light.

However, it was soon eclipsed by *Novelty*, an 0-2-2 regarded as the world's first tank engine, which reached 30mph.

The bizarre *Cycloped* hauled a short rake of wagons carrying about 50 people and reached 5mph – after which neither it nor the Winans man-powered engine took any further part in the proceedings.

Novelty was first to run on October 7, but after reaching 20¾mph on a loaded run, its bellows burst and it was stopped.

The first serious time trials took place on October 8 when *Rocket* made 40 separate journeys, reaching a maximum speed of 29mph and an average of 16mph.

Friday, October 9 saw Hackworth steam *Sans Pareil*. Some said that Stephenson was so impressed by the more efficient blast that was produced by *Sans Pareil* because of the single exhaust pipe entering its chimney that he had one immediately made in Warrington for *Rocket* and had it fitted overnight.

The next day saw *Novelty* on trial, but on the first return journey when the engineman closed the cock between the feed pump and the boiler, the resulting water pressure burst the feed pipe.

While it was away for repairs in Prescot two miles away, and in its absence, Stephenson brought out *Rocket* again, complete with modified blastpipe, and reached 30mph during two runs without either its tender or load.

The trials resumed on Tuesday,

October 13 when *Sans Pareil*, which had been previously hampered by boiler leakage, entered the fray, despite being heavier than the stipulated limit of 4½ tons and reached speeds of around 14mph. however, on its 16th trip the feed pumps failed, causing the water level in the boiler to fall to 8in and the leaden plug to melt. After repairs were carried out, the force pump failed again, and it was withdrawn from the trials.

After three days were spent dismantling and reassembling *Novelty*, it returned to the trials on October 14, but during its second trip that day, a boiler joint blew and it was withdrawn.

Perseverance made several experimental runs but could reach only 6mph, and *Burstall*, realising it would be wholly unsuitable for the Liverpool & Manchester Railway, also bowed out.

No, it didn't win the Rainhill Trials: a replica of the equine-powered contraption *Cycloped* in the 2002 'replay' of the event at the Llangollen Railway. PAUL APPLETON

This 'version' of John Ericsson and John Braithwaite's Rainhill entrant 0-2-2 *Novelty* was assembled in 1929 using many original parts, and is displayed in the Museum of Science & Industry in Manchester. It is also part of the National Collection. MOSI

THE WINNER!

Rocket's last run was its finest hour. On the final day of the trials, it pulled a carriage containing 25 passengers up an inclined plane at a speed of 20mph.

The prize was duly awarded to the owners of *Rocket*, George Stephenson, his son Robert, and Henry Booth. A pipe, which had been smoked by Sir Walter Raleigh just before his execution, was presented to George Stephenson in honour of his achievement.

Accordingly, the Liverpool & Manchester bought *Rocket* there and then and also offered to buy *Sans Pareil* and *Novelty*.

Hackworth, who was always desperately short of money, accepted the £550 offer but Braithwaite and Ericsson turned it down believing that they could hone *Novelty* to perfection and win many orders for what during the trials had been a huge success in terms of public appeal.

The remains of the original *Sans Pareil* are housed in the Locomotion museum at Shildon, which also has a

Robert Stephenson, George's son, who is now believed by many to have had a far greater part in the design of *Rocket* than had traditionally been accepted.

1980-built working replica. Both are also part of the National Collection.

George Stephenson had designed several locomotives before but none had been anything nearly as advanced as *Rocket*. It marked a watershed between the pioneer steam locomotives of the likes of Trevithick, Blenkinsop and Hackworth, and those of the world-shrinking Railway Age to come.

Indeed, *Rocket* was far more revolutionary than the likes of Oliver Cromwell, Karl Marx or Fidel Castro could ever be, for in a single package it brought together several innovations to produce the most advanced locomotive of its day, and an important stage in an evolving design of Stephenson's locomotives that set the pattern for most steam engines in the following 150 years.

Rocket had a tall chimney at the front with a blastpipe, and a multi-tube boiler with a separate firebox. The large single pair of wooden wheels was driven directly by two external cylinders set at an angle, producing for the first time a fast, light locomotive of only moderate hauling power. *Rocket* duly became the first 0-2-2 and first single-driver locomotive.

It was subsequently modified so that the cylinders were set close to horizontal, which was to become the norm for nearly all subsequent steam designs. The firebox capacity was enlarged and the shape simplified; and the locomotive was given a drum smokebox.

These arrangements can be seen in the engine as preserved today. The Engineer magazine said in 1884: "It seems to us indisputable that the *Rocket* of 1829 and 1830 were totally different engines".

A contemporary sketch of *Rocket* in its early years, from Lives of the Engineers by Samuel Smiles.

TRAGEDY STRIKES

September 15, 1830 was named as the day of the official opening of the Liverpool & Manchester Railway, and as would be expected, drew enormous crowds.

The chief guest was the Tory prime minister, Arthur Wellesley, the first of Duke of Wellington, who had agreed to open the railway. Three special carriages had been built for the occasion, with the most magnificent of them for the duke.

Just before 10am as he arrived, a band played See, the Conquering Hero Comes in praise of his victory over Napoleon at Waterloo. The rendition started a tradition of the song being played at almost every British railway station opening from then on.

The duke's party boarded their carriage before a gun was then fired to mark the official opening of the railway.

Northumbrian, the last of Stephenson's *Rocket*-style 0-2-2s, hauled the duke's train, driven by George Stephenson. The others were led by *No. 6 Phoenix*, driven by Robert Stephenson.

Northumbrian was the first locomotive to have the Stephenson-type firebox incorporated in the boiler, and have a smokebox the full diameter of the boiler, as such it had the first true 'locomotive' boiler, and took the development of the steam locomotive on one step further than the Rainhill Trials victor. It also had plate frames, a proper tender, and the cylinders set at a relatively low angle to the horizontal, giving smoother running.

An unwanted world first took place 13 miles out of Liverpool. One of the trains derailed and the train behind collided with it. The concept of train paths and leaving sufficient distance between them was clearly in its embryonic stage. It was the first-ever collision between two passenger trains, but worse was to follow.

Later that day, the locomotives stopped at the midway point of Parkside station, half a mile east of Newton-le-Willows and 17 miles from Liverpool, to take on water, 55mins after departure.

Railway officials told passengers to stay on board while the locomotives'

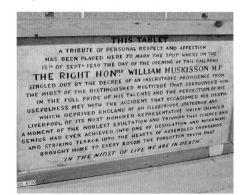

This memorial tablet was erected at the spot where William Huskisson was hit by *Rocket*, itself part of the National Collection, and housed in the National Railway Museum at York. REINHASRD DIETRICH

Crowds gather to watch the official opening of the Liverpool & Manchester Railway.

An early Liverpool & Manchester Railway train powers through Olive Mount cutting.

tanks were replenished, but this instruction was quickly forgotten when the special train carrying the Duke of Wellington also stopped, and about 50 VIPS alighted to pay their respects.

Among them was Liverpool MP William Huskisson, president of the Board of Trade and treasurer of the Navy, who had worked hard to make the Liverpool & Manchester Railway a reality. Weakened by a serious illness, he had felt it was his duty to attend the opening day.

Huskisson had argued with Wellington in 1828 over the issue of parliamentary reform and resigned from the cabinet.

However, he wanted to become friends with the duke again, and was called to one side by William Holmes, the Tory chief whip. He said that the duke had been put in a particularly good mood by the cheering crowds lining the route, and it might be an opportune moment for Huskisson and the duke to attempt the sought-for reconciliation.

So, Huskisson approached the duke's carriage and shook his hand. He was so elated at his reception by the prime minister that he did not notice that *Rocket* was approaching on the parallel track.

Onlookers shouted warnings, but *Rocket* could not be stopped in time, for as it was an engineering prototype it did not have any brakes. All the driver could do was to throw the locomotive into reserve gear, a process that took 10 seconds.

Huskisson and Holmes realised the danger too late and panicked. Holmes clung to the side of the duke's carriage, but after making two vain attempts to run across the tracks to safety, Huskisson found himself pressed against the side of the carriage and tried in vain to climb inside.

While trying to leap through the carriage door, Huskinson misjudged the distance and grabbed the doorhandle, but it swung open leaving him hanging directly in the path of the oncoming *Rocket*. The engine hit the door and Huskisson fell on to the tracks in front of the oncoming train, suffering extremely serious leg injuries.

Northumbrian was hurriedly detached from the special to take Huskisson to hospital, in doing so, forming the world's first ambulance train, which reached a speed of 35mph. The MP was taken to the vicarage at Eccles and placed in the care of the wife of the vicar, Rev Thomas Blackburne, while George Stephenson drove *Northumbrian* on to Manchester with Lord Wilton, after uncoupling the trailing musicians' carriage, he then collected four surgeons, who returned to Eccles riding on the tender.

Despite the best efforts that could be made on the spot, the MP died in the vicarage at 8.45pm after changing his will in favour of his wife Emily, who witnessed much of the tragedy.

Had Huskisson stood where he was when he saw Rocket approaching, he would have been safe; it was his panic that led to his death.

Despite a popular misconception, the MP was not the first railway fatality: the earliest recorded death caused by a steam locomotive was that of an unnamed woman, described as, 'a blind American beggar', who was fatally injured by a train on the Stockton & Darlington Railway on March, 5 1827. However, Huskisson's death was the first to be widely reported. His widow, Emily, died in 1856, never again having travelled by train.

RELEGATED TO OBSCURITY

It must be remembered that *Rocket* had been built solely to prove a point, and to win a contest first and foremost, rather than to run in regular traffic for many years.

George Stephenson immediately followed up on the 0-2-2 types with the successful 2-2-0 *Planet* of 1830, which had internal front-mounted cylinders set to the horizontal. Engines built to the *Planet* design and the subsequent 2-2-2 *Patentee* type of 1833 quickly rendered *Rocket's* design obsolete.

In 1834, *Rocket* was chosen for further (unsuccessful) modifications to test a newly developed rotary steam engine designed by Lord Dundonald.

It cylinders and driving rods were removed and two of the engines were installed directly on its driving axle with a feedwater pump in between.

On October 22 that year, trials proved disappointing, with *Rocket* unable to pull a train of empty carriages.

In 1836, *Rocket* was sold for £300 and began service on the Brampton Railway, a mineral line in Cumberland.

In 1862, the locomotive was donated to the Patent Office Museum in London (now the Science Museum) by the Thompsons of Milton Hall, near Brampton.

Rocket is now displayed in the Science Museum in London, but in a form greatly altered from its appearance in the Rainhill Trials.

In December 2015, *Rocket* appeared on the pages of the new UK passport, pictured on the Sankey Viaduct bridge in Newton-le-Willows.

Known also as the Nine Arches, the bridge forms part of the Liverpool & Manchester Railway.

The 1979-built working replica of Stephenson's *Rocket*, now in the care of the National Railway Museum, heads towards Loughborough during the Great Central Railway's 'Golden Oldies' gala on June 1, 2010. ROBIN JONES

IMITATION – THE BEST FORM OF FLATTERY

The immortal fame of *Rocket* is such that several replicas have been built, not just in Britain but overseas.

A replica of *Rocket* was produced around 1904, for the 75th anniversary of the Rainhill Trials, and appeared on a postcard issued by the London & North Western Railway, which had inherited the Liverpool & Manchester through mergers. However, little more is known about this replica, or its fate.

Hollywood stepped in when working

a replica was built in 1923 for the Buster Keaton silent movie, Our Hospitality, and also appeared in the film, The Iron Mule, two years later. Its fate is also unknown.

In 1929, Robert Stephenson & Hawthorns was commissioned to build two replicas for motor-car magnate Henry Ford. Both are now static exhibits, one at the Henry Ford Museum in the Detroit suburb of Dearborn, while the other is at the Museum of Science and Industry in Chicago.

In 1935, a very impressive cutaway static replica was built for display

alongside the original Rocket in London's Science Museum. This bright yellow-liveried one is the replica that today is one of the most popular exhibits in the Great Hall at the National Railway Museum in York, standing as it does at the front of a pair of replica Liverpool & Manchester carriages.

Better was to follow. In 1979, a fully working replica of *Rocket* was built by engineer Mike Satow and his Locomotion Enterprises for the Rocket 150 anniversary celebrations at Rainhill. It was displayed in London's Kensington Gardens on the 150th anniversary of the trials.

A frequent and hugely popular visitor to heritage railways, it was fitted with a chimney shorter than the original in order to the clear the bridge at Rainhill, where there is now less headroom than when the line was built in the 1820s.

The Rocket 150 event took place on the Liverpool & Manchester route, and a working replica of *Novelty* was also built by Locomotive Enterprises, at the preserved Bowes Railway in County Durham.

The Rainhill Trials were 'restaged' at the Llangollen Railway in 2002 for the BBC TV programme, Timewatch: Rocket and its Rivals, using modern-day replicas, including the *Novelty* replica, which returned to the UK especially for the event after having been sold to the Swedish Railway Museum in Gävle in 1982. An earlier 'replica' of *Novelty*, which is on static display in the Museum

The 1979-built replica of *Rocket* being rebuilt at he Flour Mill workshops at Bream, into a new version of the same locomotive! BILL PARKER

As well as Timothy Hackworth's original, the Locomotion museum also has this 1980-built working replica of *Sans Pareil*. ROBIN JONES

of Science & Industry in Manchester, includes parts from the original and dates from 1929. It too is part of the National Collection.

The Timewatch event used Mike Satow's replica of *Rocket* and, running alongside new-build versions of the original entrants, again won the contest.

Building replicas of steam locomotives is nowadays nothing new, the market leader being The A1 Steam Locomotive Trust's Peppercorn A1 Pacific No. 60163 *Tornado*.

However, the 1979 working replica of *Rocket* differs from all the others – because it has been built twice.

In 2009 it was completely rebuilt by the Victorian locomotive restoration experts at chartered surveyor and globetrotting steam aficionado Bill Parker's Flour Mill Colliery workshops at Bream in the Forest of Dean.

There, it was fitted not only with a new boiler, but also new frames, the component that gives a locomotive its identity. The 'new new' *Rocket* replica returned to steam in February 2010, and continues to entertain crowds wherever it goes.

The static replica inside the Great Hall looks across the turntable to A4 Pacific No. 4468 *Mallard*. ROBIN JONES

The Science Museum's 1935-built static and cutaway *Rocket* replica is one of the star exhibits in the Great Hall of the National Railway Museum at York, as pictured on April 23, 2017. ROBIN JONES

Chapter 2

CORNWALL

The second-generation steam machine!

When Richard Trevithick gave the first public demonstration of a steam railway locomotive in 1804, there was no national rail network. The railways that existed were little local affairs, worked by horses, to serve mines and other industrial sites. However, fast forward, just over four decades, and his son Francis built a showpiece locomotive for the great trunk railway that linked the Midlands to the North-West.

Richard Trevithick gave the world rapid transit, in the form of the steam railway locomotive.

It never made him any money. He died penniless at the age of 62 in Dartford, and never lived to see the first public steam railway in Cornwall, the Bodmin & Wadebridge Railway, open a year later.

It is barely possible to calculate the extent to which this son of a Cornish mining captain reshaped the globe, and created the basic tools that formed the modern age in which we live. His most significant contribution was the development of the first high-pressure steam engine. Railways led on to steamships, cars, aircraft, and then space rockets.

However, he did not only leave a legacy in terms of transport technology. His son and descendants also carried on the great steam engineering tradition that he had started.

His son Francis was born in 1812 and 20 years later, began studying civil engineering. In 1840, Francis was taken on by the Grand Junction Railway, which linked Liverpool and Manchester to Birmingham, and subsequently became part of the LNWR.

When the LNWR was formed in 1846, it was split into Northern, North Eastern and Southern divisions, corresponding to the former Grand Junction, Manchester & Birmingham and London & Birmingham railways respectively. Francis Trevithick became locomotive superintendent of the Northern Division.

In the 1840s, as railways aimed to reduce travelling times by means of faster locomotives, the trend was for them to be built with a large central driving wheel, of around 8ft diameter. The design required a low centre of

LNWR 2-2-2 No. 3020 *Cornwall* on display inside the Locomotion museum at Shildon. ROBIN JONES

BELOW: *Cornwall* as rebuilt by John Ramsbottom in 1858.

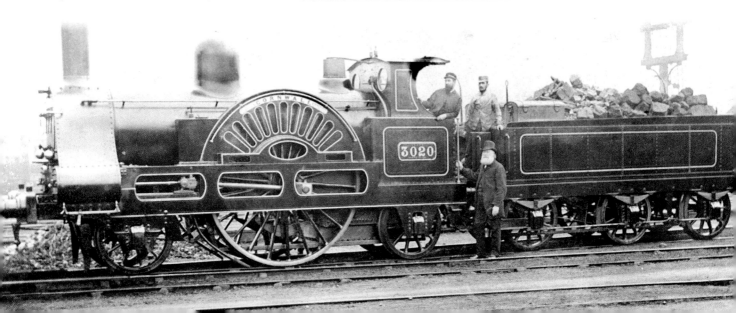

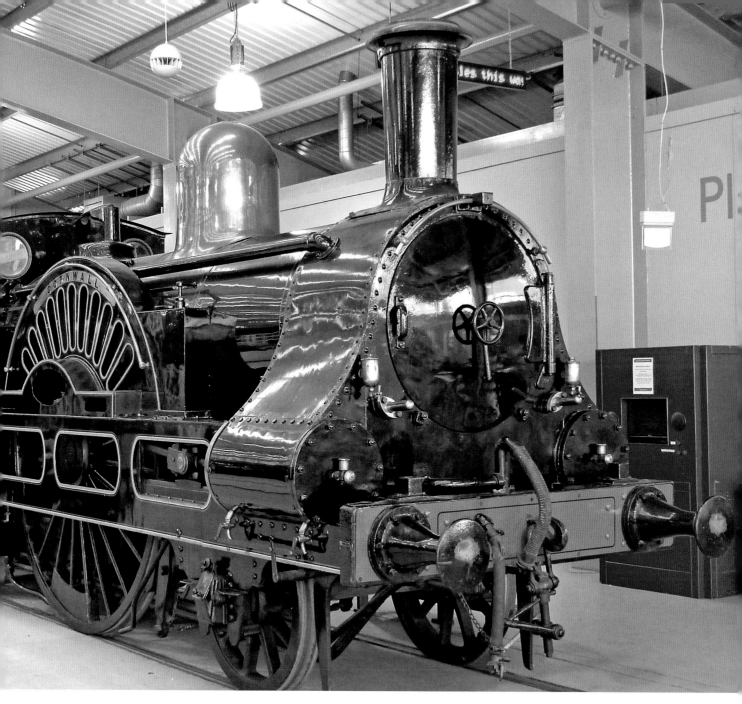

gravity, and early locomotives of this type accordingly were fitted with low-slung boilers, but this led to a conflict between the driving axle and boiler positions.

Engineer, Thomas Russell Crampton, placed the single driving axle behind the firebox, so that the driving wheels could be huge. The net result was a long locomotive, often with a 6-2-0 wheel arrangement. One of the Cramptons supplied to the LNWR, named *Liverpool*, could certainly work heavy trains at speed, but its long rigid frame damaged the track.

Francis Trevithick overcame the problem with the design of his 4-2-2 of 1847, No. 173 *Cornwall*, named after the delectable duchy, where the global transport revolution can be said to have begun thanks to his father.

Francis moved the driving axle ahead of the firebox, giving a shorter overall wheelbase, and positioned the boiler beneath the driving axle. *Cornwall* was exhibited at the Great Exhibition of

1851, but was extensively rebuilt under the LNWR's engineer John Ramsbottom, and became a more conventional 2-2-2 in 1858. A less-drastic rebuild in the 1870s saw *Cornwall* acquire a typical LNWR cab, and a new number, 3020, was allocated in June 1886.

Cornwall was a very successful express engine of its period, and known to have achieved 70mph down Whitmore bank near Crewe in 1884. It was withdrawn from express service on the Liverpool-Manchester route in 1902 but was then used to haul the mechanical engineer's inspection coach into early LMS days.

In view of its longevity, on retirement, *Cornwall* was preserved by the LMS, and normally retained at Crewe Works, although occasionally exhibited in public. It was finally placed on permanent public display in the Museum of British Transport at Clapham on December 16, 1962. On closure of the short-lived museum, it returned to Crewe Works in 1975.

Cornwall spent a period on loan to the Severn Valley Railway as a static exhibit from August 16, 1979 to September 15, 1983 when it finally made it to the National Railway Museum at York.

It is currently on display inside the Locomotion museum in Shildon.

After leaving the LNWR, Francis returned to Cornwall and became factor of the Tehidy estates, of which his grandfather had been mineral agent in the 18th century.

He wrote a biography of his father, which was published in 1872. He died at Penzance on October 27, 1877 and was buried there.

His son, Arthur Reginald Trevithick (1858-1939), worked for many years on the LNWR, including several years as assistant locomotive works manager at Crewe.

Another son, Frederick Harvey Trevithick (1852-1931), worked for both the GWR and the Egyptian State Railways where he advanced to Chief Mechanical Engineer.

GREAT NORTHERN No.1
The first of the East Coast speed kings

When Patrick Stirling was appointed to the Great Northern Railway as locomotive superintendent in 1866, speed was his ultimate goal, and the most famous of his products were the legendary Stirling Single 4-2-2s, which paved the way for ever-shorter journeys between London and Edinburgh.

GNR Stirling single 4-2-2 No. 1 accelerates away from Loughborough on the Great Central Railway on Saturday, May 8, 1982. BRIAN SHARPE

Patrick Stirling was born in Kilmarnock in 1820 and came from a family with a proven track record in steam engineering.

His father, Rev Robert Stirling had, in 1816, invented the first practical example of a closed cycle air engine; and to that came to be known as a Stirling engine.

His brother, James Stirling, was also a locomotive engineer, while Patrick's son Matthew became Chief Mechanical Engineer of the Hull & Barnsley Railway.

Patrick Stirling was taken on as an apprentice at Urquhart Lindsay & Company's Dundee Foundry and subsequently became foreman at Neilson's Locomotive Works in Glasgow.

In 1851, he became superintendent of a

short line between Bowling and Balloch, which was later taken over the North British Railway.

Two years later, he was made locomotive superintendent of the Glasgow & South Western Railway where he stayed for 13 years.

His finest hour, however, came at the GNR, where he stayed in charge until his death in 1895.

On his arrival at the GNR, Stirling set out to standardise the railway's rolling stock as there had been little standardisation under his predecessor, Archibald Sturrock.

He borrowed a 'single-wheeler' from the Great Eastern Railway and, in 1868, designed two versions of a 2-2-2 with 7ft 1in driving wheels.

His aim was to produce a fleet of standard engines that combined speed with power in order to tackle the continuous gradients on the King's Cross to York line.

The GER designs were developed specifically for the GNR's high-speed expresses. Stirling used outside cylinders and a 4-2-2 wheel arrangement for stability at the front end.

These were key steps in the evolution of the design of the Stirling Single, with the first appearing from Doncaster Works in 1870 followed by another 52 between then and 1895.

He disliked the concept of compound engines, and preferred traditional types with outside cylinders and domeless boilers.

His Stirling Single 4-4-2s were designed for express passenger work on the GNR. With a single pair of 8ft 1in diameter driving wheels, and nicknamed 'eight footers', they were intended to haul up to 26 coaches at an average speed of 47mph. In short, they became distinctive images of Victorian railway technology at its finest and fastest.

The first was numbered 1. The GNR

did not follow the practice of other lines in having a sequence of numbers for set classes: if a locomotive was scrapped, its number was up for grabs.

Designed especially for high-speed express trains from King's Cross, they cemented the GNR's reputation for speed.

For many years the Stirling Singles were, as an overall class, the fastest locomotives in England, and indeed the world. Their designer became a living legend among engineers and enthusiasts alike, and through him the GNR became one of the most popular routes in the country.

The GNR never tried to hide the fact that it ran fast expresses. This approach was the opposite of most other British companies of the day, which were mindful of the public concerns about high speed and the resulting increased likelihood of crashes.

Stirling also established the locomotive works at Doncaster so that

Stirling Single No. 1 at King's Cross top shed on September 11, 1938 ready to back down on to a vintage six-wheeler train set that is waiting in the station to take Railway Correspondence and Travel Society members on the first-ever privately organised railtour, to Peterborough. Around this time, the celebrity locomotive also made other trips including a day excursion to Cambridge.

The second half of the 1930s were a momentous time for the LNER, with the success of the 'Silver Jubilee', 'Coronation', 'West Riding Limited' named trains and A4 No. 4468 *Mallard's* 126mph world record, plus in 1938 a completely new train set for the 'Flying Scotsman' including the new concept of a buffet lounge car with ladies retiring room, which survives and can be seen at Kirkby Stephen East on the Stainmore Railway in Cumbria. The whole train was pressure-ventilated and double glazed.

The main reason why Stirling Single No. 1 was brought out of retirement was to promote this new train, with journalists being taken in East Coast Joint Stock six-wheeler stock hauled by No. 1 as far as Stevenage, to represent a 'Scotsman' train of the 1870s.

The passengers were then transferred to the new 1938 stock for onward transit. The train not only had Sir Nigel Gresley on board, but was also hauled by his namesake A4 4498. ERIC FRY COLLECTION

the GNR could start to build its own engines, and it was there that his Singles were built.

It was not the only locomotive type that he built for the GNR; there were 2-2-2s for express passenger duties, 2-4-0s and 0-4-2s for branch passenger train and mixed traffic, 0-4-4Ts for suburban passenger trains, 0-6-0s for freight and 0-6-0Ts for shunting.

However, it is the Stirling Single for which he is readily remembered. Its prowess and fleet-footedness were never more underlined than in the two escapades in late Victorian times, which came to be known as the Races to the North.

On August 20, 1895, in the second Race to the North held at night between the operators of the east and west coast route from London to Scotland, Stirling Single 4-2-2 No. 668 took the East Coast express 105½-miles from King's Cross to Grantham in one hour 41mins with an average speed of 62.7mph. An engine change saw No. 775 take over, and complete the 82 miles to York in one hour 16min; an average speed of 64.7mph.

The overall 393-mile trip was covered in six hours 19mins, at a speed of 63.5 mph, while the extended run to Aberdeen, making a total of 523 miles, took eight hours 40 minutes, with an average speed 60.4 mph.

With the arrival of the Ivatt Atlantics after 1898, the Singles began to be displaced from express services, and withdrawals of the early engines, which had become an icon of Victorian transport technology at its finest, began in 1899, but the last ones were used on secondary services until 1916.

A star-studded line up at King's Cross shed in September 1938: left to right are Stirling Single No. 1; GNR J3 0-6-0 No. 4039; GNR C1 Atlantic No. 4-4-2 No. 4404; A3 Pacific No. 2505 *Cameronian* and A4 Pacific No. 4462 *Great Snipe*. ERIC FRY COLLECTION

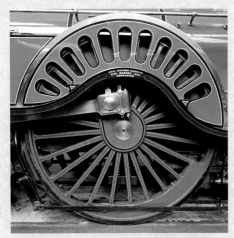

The single most distinctive feature of the Stirling Single: the 8ft 1in driving wheel that made them speed kings of the Victorian age. ROBIN JONES

Stirling Single No. 1 heads a train of teak coaches at the Doncaster Works open day in 2003. ROBIN JONES

A STAR IN A SECOND LIFE TOO

The first of the class, No 1, was preserved by the LNER on withdrawal in 1907, firstly at King's Cross shed. It was displayed at an exhibition in Wembley in 1909, and then stored at Doncaster Works.

The public saw it occasionally and it took part in the 1925 Stockton & Darlington centenary cavalcade in steam, after the LNER gave it a new boiler.

This centenary led to the establishment of the York Railway Museum by the LNER and No. 1 was placed there on permanent public display.

It emerged in 1938 to take part in the LNER's publicity programme, hauling a GNR train on the GN main line, and also featuring in railtours, becoming the first preserved British steam locomotive to haul a main line passenger train.

It returned to the museum where it remained until its closure in 1974, after which it moved to the new National Railway Museum. A surprise was the decision to return it to steam, after which it ran for just three weekends on the Great Central Railway in 1981-82.

It also took part in a filming session on the North Yorkshire Moors Railway at Levisham and there was even talk of a main line run to Scarborough. Sadly, that proved to be too ambitious.

No. 1 is now display at the National Railway Museum in York.

In 1898, an 18in gauge model of No. 1 was built by students at London's Regent Street Polytechnic. They included Henry Greenly who found fame as a builder of similar miniature locomotives for lines such as the Romney, Hythe & Dymchurch Railway. The scaled-down Stirling single was sold to EFS Notter, who was the GNR's district locomotive superintendent based at King's Cross, and who later kept it in King's shed; home of the full-size originals. After changing hands several times, the locomotive is now at the World of Country Life Museum at Sandy Bay, Exmouth.

In 2010, No. 1 starred in a critically acclaimed stage production of Edith A Nesbit's children's classic, The Railway Children, at the redundant Waterloo International platform. Shunted into position during the performances by a Class 08 diesel, a fog machine was used to generate the smoke effects. ROBIN JONES

Stirling Single No. 1 displayed inside the Great Hall of the National Railway Museum at York in January 2017. ROBIN JONES

HARDWICKE

The great late Victorian racehorse

At a time when the public was excited by the prospect of faster trains, and the railways were shrinking the world, LNWR 'Improved Precedent' No. 790 *Hardwicke* certainly delivered the goods.

By late Victorian times, train travel had long become an accepted part of everyday life, and it was no longer a novelty to complete a journey that previously took several days by road in just a few hours. Emphasis shifted towards how quickly that journey could be undertaken.

As passenger comfort increased, so did the demand for speed as well as rivalry between companies serving the same destination. Nowhere was this rivalry as intense as between the operators of what we call today the East and West Coast main lines.

The Races to the North was the name bestowed by the press to occasions in the summers of 1888 and 1895 in which these operators raced trains from London to Scotland. Such "races" were never official and publicly the companies denied that what happened was in fact racing at all.

The big star of the 1895 race was Francis William Webb's LNWR Precedent 2-4-0 No. 790 *Hardwicke*.

Webb, who replaced John Ramsbottom as the LNWR's Chief Mechanical Engineer in 1871 was one of Britain's best-known 19th-century locomotive engineers.

In 1851, aged 15, he became an articled pupil of Francis Trevithick at Crewe Works, rising to works manager at Crewe by 1861 under Ramsbottom. After a period at a steelmakers in Bolton, in October 1870, Webb was appointed as

LNWR Locomotive Superintendent, a position that was soon redesignated as Chief Mechanical Engineer.

He introduced some very successful standard locomotive classes, large numbers of which built at Crewe. He was also responsible for the remodelling of Crewe station, which involved four-track underpasses to carry freight traffic.

Webb designed the 'Improved' or 'Renewed' Precedent express 2-4-0, and 160 were built at Crewe between 1887 and 1902. Officially, they were rebuilds of earlier types, the 96 Newtons and the 80 Precedents, but in effect this was merely a paper exercise for the accountants, and they were new builds in all but name – as they retained the names and numbers of the locomotives they had replaced.

The Improved Precedents were not only capable of high speeds but regularly hauled heavy loads in relation to their small size, hence their nickname of 'Jumbo'.

The race involved night expresses running between London and Aberdeen. The finishing post was Kinnaber Junction, 38 miles south of Aberdeen, where the Caledonian Railway and the North British Railway routes joined before running into the Granite City over Caledonian metals.

The two routes ran either side of Montrose Basin on the approach to the junction, and journalists covering the races could see their train racing against the other.

On August 20, the Great Northern Railway's Stirling Single 4-2-2 No. 668 took the East Coast express 105.5-miles from King's Cross to Grantham in 1hr 41mins with an average speed of 62.7mph.

An engine change saw sister No. 775 take over, and complete the 82 miles to York in 1hr 16mins, an average speed of 64.7mph.

The overall 393-mile trip was covered in 6hrs 19mins, at a speed of 63.5mph, while the extended run to Aberdeen, a total of 523 miles, took 8hrs 40mins, with an average speed of 60.4 mph.

Definitely and defiantly not to be beaten, the LNWR responded two days later with a storming run by Improved Precedent or 'Jumbo' express passenger 2-4-0 No. 790 *Hardwicke* that took 2hrs and 6mins to cover the 141 miles from Crewe to Carlisle, reaching 88mph in places, with an average speed of 67.1mph, setting a new speed record in the Races to the North. The record has never been bettered over the route by steam.

Francis Webb, who was once regarded as the 'King of Crewe', designed the 'Improved Precedents'.

The Improved Precedents were designed by Francis Webb and built at Crewe Works, 166 in batches between 1887-97, and two more in 1898 and 1901. They were among the most famous British steam locomotives of the 19th century.

Even more famous in its day than *Hardwicke* was No. 955 *Charles Dickens*, which hauled the 8.30am express from Manchester to Euston and the 4pm return for 20 years. In doing so it clocked up more than two million miles, a record that has never been broken by any other British steam locomotive.

Yet again, steam was shrinking the world, in the decade before the Wright brothers made their first flights.

However, in June 1896, the rivals negotiated a minimum journey time for the Anglo-Scottish trains to reduce the possibility of danger at excessive speeds, but the agreement applied only to daytime services and not those running at night, as in the races.

As stated elsewhere, a fatal accident at Preston station on July 13, 1896 ended any thoughts of resuming the Race to the North, at least in Victorian times and for some decades afterwards.

The 8pm Down 'Highland Express' from Euston to Scotland derailed to the north of Preston station at night, killing one passenger, but turning the public against the idea of ever-faster express trains.

Withdrawals of the Improved Precedents started in December 1905, but 76 members of the class survived into LMS days. One class member, *Snowdon*, by then numbered 5001, lasted until 1934 when it had to be renumbered 25001 as a new Stanier 'Black Five' 4-6-0 had been allocated No. 5001.

A unique pre-Grouping National Collection double-header on the main line. LNWR 'Improved Precedent' 2-4-0 No. 790 *Hardwicke* and Midland Railway compound 4-4-0 No. 1000 depart from Poppleton near York on April 24, 1976.
BRIAN SHARPE

Improved Precedent 2-4-0 No. 790 *Hardwicke* at Crewe, with the driver and fireman who made the record run to Aberdeen in the Race to the North on August 22, 1895.
BRITISH RAILWAYS

No. 790 *Hardwicke* inside the Locomotion museum at Shildon. ROBIN JONES

Hardwicke taking part in the Rocket 150 cavalcade at Rainhill in 1980. BARRY LEWIS*

TOO FAMOUS TO SCRAP

Hardwicke, which carried the LMS number 5031, was a late withdrawal in 1932 and was one of a very select number of historic engines that even the LMS did not feel should be scrapped.

It was sidelined at Crewe Works but very rarely saw the light of day until it was put on display in the new Museum of British Transport at Clapham in 1962.

However, when Clapham closed after a few years in preparation for the opening of the National Railway Museum at York, *Hardwicke* was not moved to York but instead on August 4, 1974, went to the former Steamtown museum at Carnforth, a bastion of early main line preservation, where it was returned to steam in July 1975 after more than 40 years.

This move was to enable it to take part in the Rail 150 Stockton & Darlington cavalcade at Shildon on August 31, 1975, but it was fully main line certified and after a test run up the Cumbrian Coast on July 22 in driving rain with a GER coach, *Hardwicke* set off for Shildon on August 17 piloting No. 4472 *Flying Scotsman*, this time with a Caledonian coach.

Following the cavalcade, *Hardwicke* took its place in the York museum. However, even greater things were to come, and it returned to Carnforth on April 24, 1976, this time piloting Midland compound 4-4-0 No. 1000 on a railtour from York. During this period it was allocated TOPS number 98190.

After that, *Hardwicke* had further outings on the Cumbrian Coast including solo shuttles from Carnforth to Grange-over-Sands and returned to York in June piloting BR Standard 9F 2-10-0 No. 92220 *Evening Star*.

A quieter existence then followed for the engine, but it was still steamed and

Hardwicke on display outside during the National Railway Museum's Railfest 2012 event. ROBIN JONES

worked occasionally on the now-closed Derwent Valley Light Railway at York.

For its appearance in the 1980 Rocket 150 cavalcade at Rainhill, *Hardwicke* was matched with three LNWR Royal Train carriages. Sadly, in what should have been a triumphant finale double-heading the empty stock on the LNWR route across the Pennines with Stanier Pacific No. 46229 *Duchess of Hamilton*, had to be diesel hauled owing to fire risk.

Hardwicke spent the rest of 1980 at the former Dinting Railway Centre but returned to York and retired to life as a static exhibit. It is now displayed inside the Locomotion museum in Shildon.

Hardwicke's sister 'Improved Precedent' 2-4-0 No. 955 *Charles Dickens* also turned in some sparkling performances to underline exactly what the class was capable of, and set an all-time record for steam mileage. TONY HISGETT*

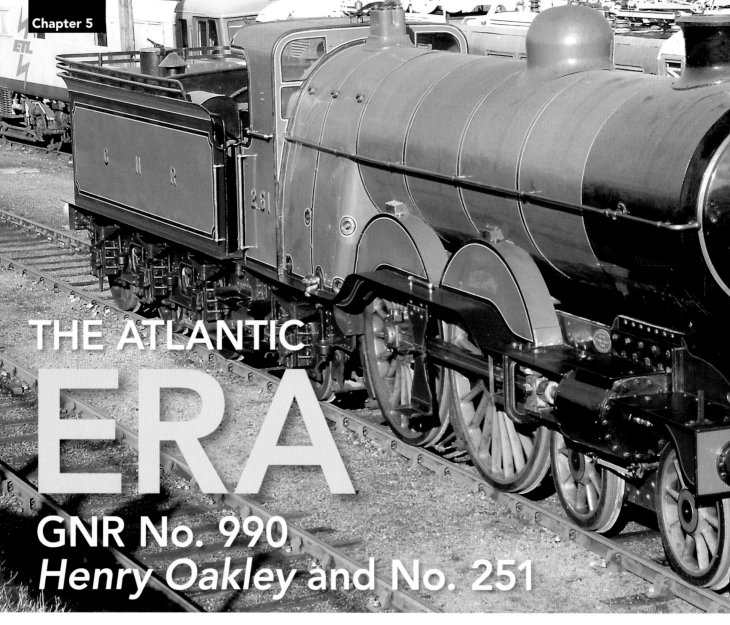

Chapter 5

THE ATLANTIC ERA
GNR No. 990 *Henry Oakley* and No. 251

The early 20th century saw the Great Northern Railway introduce the first Atlantic locomotives to Britain, rendering the powerful Stirling Singles all but obsolete.

After the Races to the North were over, the Great Northern Railway changed its emphasis from speed to style, with amenities both for first- and third-class passengers coming top of the list.

In 1899, a second rival route to the capital was opened, when the Manchester, Sheffield & Lincolnshire Railway completed its London Extension to Marylebone and became the Great Central Railway. The GNR managed to keep its King's Cross to Manchester expresses, while at the same time, there was a huge surge in demand for freight traffic. In all, the GNR found itself needing another 70 locomotives to cope.

Stirling was succeeded by Henry Alfred Ivatt, a former apprentice under John Ramsbottom at the LNWR's Crewe Works, who became Ireland's Great Southern & Western Railway's Southern District locomotive superintendent in 1877. In 1895, he became the GNR's locomotive superintendent.

He rebuilt the Stirling Singles with larger boilers and cylinders and also produced a new class of singles, which were the last to be made. They had similar front ends to the Stirling singles, and shared their driving wheel size.

He also introduced the first Atlantic locomotives to Britain. The 4-4-2 had first appeared in 1888 in the USA, as the natural development of the 4-4-0, the additional trailing truck not only supporting a larger firebox but improving the riding. The wheel arrangement became known as the Atlantic.

Henry Ivatt was also the first to introduce Walschaerts valve gear to this country. Invented by Belgian railway mechanical engineer, Egide Walschaerts, in 1844, it offered the advantage that it could be mounted entirely on the outside of a locomotive, leaving the space between the frames clear.

Whereas Stephenson valve gear remained the most commonly used valve gear on 19th-century locomotives, the Walschaerts valve gear took precedence in the 20th century.

Under Ivatt, big boilers, not massive single driving wheels and faster running, were the trend. His first engines were 4-4-0s carrying some of the largest boilers in Britain, but for him, they were not big enough.

He extended the locomotive frames and added a pair of carrying wheels so he could make the boilers even bigger, increasing their length from 10ft 1in to 13ft.

Ivatt's counterpart on the Lancashire & Yorkshire Railway John Aspinall was also working on an Atlantic and Ivatt's Atlantic was given a high priority by the GNR in order to beat the L&Y to it. Numbered 990 and named *Henry Oakley* after the GNR general manager, it was outshopped from Doncaster Works in 1898, beating Aspinall's prototype by a few months. It was the only named engine on the GNR until Gresley's first Pacific emerged in 1922.

The first production Ivatt Atlantics, known as Klondikes, entered service in 1900, and proved fast runners, sometimes having to be held back on less well-maintained sections of track.

LEFT: Great Northern Railway Ivatt C1 4-4-2 No. 251 in green livery on February 7, 2014, at Barrow Hill Roundhouse's Giant of Steam gala, Built in 1902, No. 251 was the first of this class in 1902 and immediately made a resounding impact on the railway world. It was the first engine in Britain to have a wide firebox and set the pattern for future Atlantics and Pacifics in the UK. Despite having a BR power classification of only 2P, the type could haul heavy expresses at speed and in the Second World War, they achieved impressive feats of haulage in difficult circumstances. ROBIN JONES

No. 990 *Henry Oakley* during its years on static display at Bressingham Steam Museum near Diss in Norfolk. BRESSINGHAM

GOING BIGGER

In December 1902, he built No. 251, the first of his Large Atlantics, by adapting the design and increasing the boiler diameter from 4ft 8in to 5ft 6in.

The GNR classified both types as C1, but the LNER classified the large boiler variation as C1 and the small boiler variation as C2.

The Atlantics all had tiny cylinders, and therefore their tractive effort was less than that of the Stirling Singles. However, they had better adhesion because of the extra driving wheels, and the larger boiler could hold steaming rates for longer. The need had clearly switched from faster trains to pulling bigger and heavier ones.

After Ivatt's Atlantics appeared, the Stirling Singles were relegated to very much secondary routes for a few years until all but No. 1 were withdrawn and scrapped.

Ivatt worked on developing his Atlantics, producing several different types, and modifying existing ones. His last development was the fitting of piston valves and Schmidt 18-row superheaters to the last 10 C1s that were built in 1910, not to increase power, but so he could reduce the boiler pressure and maintenance costs.

Ivatt's successor, Nigel Gresley, added 24-element superheaters from 1912 and raised the boiler pressure, later fitting 32-element superheaters. As such, Ivatt's Atlantics continued to be used on top-link duties throughout the Thirties, including the Pullman trains from King's Cross. However, only two Ivatt Atlantics survived into British Railways ownership. The last, No. 62822, was withdrawn in November 1950.

Another railway dynasty: Henry Ivatt's son, George Ivatt, became the postwar Chief Mechanical Engineer of the LMS, while his daughter Marjorie married Oliver Bulleid, CME of the Southern Railway, famous for his streamlined Pacifics. Henry Ivatt died in 1923 in Sussex.

THE TWO SURVIVORS

As LNER No. 3990, *Henry Oakley* (GNR No. 990) was withdrawn at the end of 1937, and was earmarked for preservation because of its historical importance as the first Ivatt Atlantic. It was restored to a GNR livery and placed in the York museum in January 1938.

Likewise, the first C1, No. 251, was preserved by the LNER just before Nationalisation and also displayed at York. In 1953, No. 990 was restored to running condition and ran a series of specials with C1 No. 251 celebrating the centenary of Doncaster Works. 'The Plant Centenarian' railtour from King's Cross to Doncaster was organised by a certain Retford businessman and steam enthusiast by the name of Alan Pegler... No. 251 never steamed again after 1954. However, No. 990 was steamed again in 1975 for the Stockton & Darlington 150th anniversary celebrations, before entering the National Railway Museum in 1975 as a part of the National Collection.

During the summer of 1977, Henry Oakley was loaned to the Keighley & Worth Valley Railway to haul passenger trains, but its working visit was cut short by boiler problems just before it was to travel to Doncaster Works.

It was duly hauled there by A3 Pacific No. 4472 Flying Scotsman, after which it went on show at the National Railway Museum at York. It was relocated to Bressingham Steam Museum in Norfolk in July 1997, and is now back inside the York museum. It has never been returned to steam.

No. 251 is now displayed inside the Locomotion museum at Shildon.

Britain's first 4-4-2: C1 Atlantic No. 990 *Henry Oakley* inside the National Railway Museum at York on April 23, 2017. ROBIN JONES

BEATTIE WELL TANK No. 30585
The little engine that could

Many classes of steam locomotive were rendered extinct by the evolution of transport technology, decades before anyone thought of preserving them, let alone establishing a National Collection. Yet two members of the LSWR 0298 class of Beattie well tanks designed for London suburban services survived despite the march of progress, because only they were fit for a task on a far-flung freight branch that later designs could not tackle.

I will never forget the looks on the faces of passengers waiting at London Underground's Earl's Court station for the first train of the day just after 6am on Sunday, February 26, 2012.

Automatically anticipating a fast, sleek tube train to emerge out of the darkness, a no-holds-barred steam locomotive suddenly appeared, filling the station with smoke.

The handful of people waiting on the platform instantly scurried in their pockets for mobile-phone cameras because they could not believe what they were seeing and just had to capture it for posterity.

They knew only too well that without photographic evidence, their family and friends would never believe their tale of what they had seen, perhaps thinking at best they had seen some ghost engine in that fictional tunnel, after having downed a drink or three!

Hollywood could not have done it better. It was like a scene from a sci-fi movie in which a train from a century and a half before suddenly appears out of a tunnel after a rift in time and space.

However, it was real. The locomotive, Beattie 2-4-0 well tank No. 30587, was part of a test train run to see if a steam locomotive could indeed run through the tube tunnels with their plethora of modern apparatus, without setting off fire alarms and contravening a raft of other safety measures. It was paving the way for what turned out to be an award-winning series of public steam trips interspersed between standard Underground services, which began a year later using other engines.

It was the latest escapade in an extraordinary tale of preservation, in which a vintage locomotive was not saved from the scrapman because of its historical worth, but because it and its two sisters were uniquely suited to a specific purpose, which for decades no other locomotive was deemed suitable.

The story began when Joseph Beattie came to the LSWR as assistant engineer at the age of 34 in 1838, having worked with Crewe Works founder Joseph Locke on the Grand Junction Railway. At the time, the LSWR main line ran from Waterloo to Dorchester, with branches to Salisbury, Windsor, Chertsey, Hampton Court, Gosport and Portsmouth.

In 1847, the LSWR made the bold and apparently over-adventurous step of buying the Bodmin & Wadebridge Railway, which in 1834 had become the first in Cornwall to use steam. A strange purchase indeed, as the short line was effectively on a transport 'island' more

Beattie well tank No. 30587 at the china clay depot at Penpont on the Wendfordbridge branch on August 27, 1962. COLOUR-RAIL

than 100 miles west of the company's then western railhead.

Beattie took over as locomotive engineer from JV Gooch in 1850. In his 21 years in the job he certainly made his mark on the railway industry. He became the first engineer to stop using single driving wheel express locomotives. He tried to eliminate the practice of tender-first working which had been responsible for numerous accidents… and he was among the first engineers to introduce tank engines for suburban working.

He developed a coal-burning firebox, which saved fuel costs, and further increased efficiency fed by using exhaust steam for boiler feed water heating.

He cast aside the practice of having cylinders between the locomotive frames and kept the centre line of boilers as low as possible. And improved riding was made possible by the use of extra steadying bearings on the leading axle with, in many cases, the well-tank springs controlling the floating axle boxes mounted directly on the lower slide bars.

EVOLUTION OF THE WELL TANKS
It was three months after Beattie's promotion to the senior position that he produced his first tank engine designs for London suburban traffic, the single driving wheeled Tartar class of well tank, of which six were built by Sharp in Manchester. In 1856 a slightly larger type appeared, the three-strong Minerva class of 2-4-0WT with 5ft 6in driving wheels. They were followed by three Nelson class 2-4-0WTs with 5ft driving wheels and three 'Nile' class engines with 5ft 9in driving wheels.

Each of these types marked an evolution towards what became known as the Standard well tank, with the first of what became a batch of 85. All were

built by Beyer Peacock at Gorton Works except for three constructed at Nine Elms. The first were delivered in 1863, and the last batch, which included No. 298 (BR No. 30587) in 1874.

They were a great success for more than 20 years, excelling not only on suburban trains where they replaced many tender engines, but also on country branches. There, the flexible 12ft 6in wheelbase enabled them to tackle the lightly laid permanent way and the tightest curves: examples were to be seen at Swanage, Seaton, Exmouth, Chard, Barnstaple and even on the Isle of Wight.

Beattie died of diphtheria in 1871 and was succeeded by his son William George, who carried on in the post until 1877 when he was replaced by William Adams who built bigger tank engines for suburban services and so replaced the Beattie types. He also had 31 Beattie well tanks rebuilt as tender engines.

SURVIVAL IN THE FAR WEST
Obsolete does not automatically mean useless, and while the tender engine rebuilds and most of the original well tanks were scrapped in the 1890s, three survived into the 20th century: Nos. 298, 314 (later 30585) and 329 (30586).

Although the LSWR had bought the Bodmin & Wadebridge Railway in 1847, it remained unconnected to it for nearly 40 years until 1895 when the North Cornwall Railway finally reached Wadebridge. The hitherto-isolated railway included a freight-only branch to the hamlet of Wenfordbridge on the western edge of Bodmin Moor, which was notorious for its tight curves as it negotiated the upper valley of the River Camel.

While they were declared past their sell-by date everywhere else, the ability of the Beattie well tanks to manage tight curves made them more suitable for the

The trio that was unintentionally preserved by the LSWR and Southern Railway because no other locomotives were deemed suitable for the Wenfordbridge branch: Beattie well tanks Nos. 30587/86 and 85 at Wadebridge on June 21, 1962, two months before British Railways withdrew them from traffic. RC RILEY

Wenfordbridge line than any others.

In 1893, another well tank, No. 248, was sent by sea from Southampton to work that line, being replaced by No. 298 two years later, which was able to travel to Wadebridge by rail and one of the first locomotives to use the North Cornwall line from Halwill Junction. Nos. 314 and 329 followed soon afterwards.

In 1900, LSWR mechanical engineer, Dugald Drummond, decided that they should be replaced and scrapped. However, an inspector sent from London to assess them was so impressed that he persuaded Drummond instead to have them overhauled at Nine Elms, even in preference to Drummond's new 02 0-4-4Ts (of which Calbourne on the Isle of Wight Steam Railway is the sole-surviving example).

In 1920 Chief Mechanical Engineer Robert Urie ordered replacement

THE RETURN TO LONDON

The luck of the Beattie well tanks finally ran out, but only in the dying years of steam in the South West, when in August 1962 they were eventually replaced by three GWR 1368 class 0-6-0PTs, the sole survivor of which is No. 1369 on the South Devon Railway. These, in turn, gave way to diesel shunters.

No. 30587 performed the last duty of a well tank in Cornwall on September, 8 1962, an enthusiasts' brake van special to Wenfordbridge.

Following the withdrawal of the well tanks, photographer Henry Casserley, secretary of the Stephenson Locomotive Society arranged, in conjunction with the Railway Correspondence & Travel Society, two joint rail tours from Waterloo to Windsor, Hampton Court, Chessington and Shepperton, using Nos. 30585 and 30587.

By the time No. 30587 had been withdrawn, it had clocked up 88 years' service, and 1,289,348 miles!

In drawing up plans for the National Collection in 1961, No. 30587 was designated for preservation, and eventually passed into National Railway Museum ownership.

The Bluebell Railway tried to buy one of the other two but decided it could not afford the long-term restoration costs because of their deteriorating condition, but No. 30585 was bought by the London Railway Preservation society, forerunner of the Quainton Railway Society.

Sadly, No. 30586 was cut up at Eastleigh in 1964, but many spare parts were acquired by the new owners of No. 30585, which arrived at Quainton Road station – now the Buckinghamshire Railway Centre – in late 1969.

No. 30587 eventually ended up repainted in LSWR green as No. 0298, loaned by the NRM to what is now the South Devon Railway. There, it stood for many years as the centrepiece of the Buckfastleigh museum, with the museum turning down requests for it to be returned to steam.

No. 30587 in 'as withdrawn' condition at a Brighton station open day in June 1973. HUGH LLEYWELYN*

boilers for the trio, and No. 298 (by then renumbered 0298) was reboilered at Eastleigh in 1921.

Repairs were needed again in 1930 but despite a Southern Eastern & Chatham Railway P class 0-6-0T being tried on the tortuous route by the Southern Railway two years earlier, no suitable replacements were found.

Already an anachronism by 1900, as the years passed the trio acquired near-mythical status, and many a rail enthusiast turned up at Padstow or Wadebridge in the hope of being lucky enough to catch one of the occasional passenger turns to Bodmin North worked by one of them.

On May 14, 1955, No. 30587 briefly left Cornwall to work a Railway Enthusiasts Club special from Andover Junction to Bulford Camp and back, heading a three-coach LSWR non-corridor set.

Steaming again on home territory: No. 30587 passes Bodmin General signalbox on November 6, 2002. ROBIN JONES

Back to back Beatties Nos. 30587 and 30585 at Hampton Court in London working a special on December 12, 1967. COLOUR-RAIL

ENTER THE FLOUR MILL

The story now switches to a steam locomotive restoration centre deep in the Forest of Dean.

Charted surveyor, Bill Parker, had established his Flour Mill workshops in former colliery buildings near the village of Bream, and having first worked with the NRM in 1990, had built up a country-wide reputation for quality workmanship, which is second to none.

He became acquainted with the Bodmin & Wenford Railway, the modern-day successor to the Bodmin & Wadebridge – when he rebuilt GWR pannier tank N. 4612 on behalf of its owners before it was sold to the Bodmin & Wenford Trust. He struck up a working partnership with retired London banker, Alan Moore, the line's principal benefactor, who held fond memories of travelling over it during his National Service in BR days.

While celebrating the arrival of No. 4612 to Bodmin General, Bill suggested to Alan that the only thing he could do to top the pannier would be to sponsor the restoration of the NRM's Beattie well tank.

Alan's response was such that Bill was soon in York, trying to persuade the NRM of the advantages of having such a wonderful ambassador for the museum in Cornwall 'where it belonged'. After the NRM agreed that under the right terms, and if the engine was sufficiently sound, it would permit the Flour Mill to restore it, Alan readily agreed to sponsor the work.

So in December 2001, the well tank was freed from long-term incarceration at Buckfastleigh and taken to the Flour Mill for exploratory work. A decision was soon reached that it could run again without major surgery, and work commenced in earnest in early 2002.

After the work began, Bill persuaded the Buckinghamshire Railway Centre to let him have the boiler of No. 30585

for overhaul too, and to cut a long story short, the Flour Mill also returned that to steam.

That autumn, No. 30587 was delivered by low loader to Bodmin General for running-in tests.

I had the honour of being on its first trip, on November 9, 2002, when No. 30587 hauled a single brake van to Boscarne, where the Wenfordbridge branch – which closed in 1983 –diverged from the Bodmin to Padstow line, and back again.

The tests were a huge success, and the little Beattie brought crowds flocking back to north Cornwall just as it had done half a century before. Not only that, in the years that followed, it became a popular guest at other heritage railways across the country.

Geoff Silcock (pictured) of photo charter organiser Sentimental Journeys organised the first event starring No. 30587 soon after its test run was complete, providing the transfers for the logo and numbers, even borrowing the appropriate headcode disc with the original BR paper numbers. The charter featuring a rake of preserved china clay wagons was fully booked within three days, such was the reception to the well tank's comeback November 2002 comeback. ROBIN JONES

BENEATH ITS FIRST HOME TERRITORY

Around 2010, London Transport Museum and the Underground began talks about how best to celebrate the 150th anniversary of the Metropolitan Railway, the world's first subterranean system, in 2013. One idea quickly snowballed: as the first Metropolitan Railway trains had been hauled by steam, why not run a Victorian steam train through the tunnels beneath the city centre?

The Steam on the Met series of the Eighties and Nineties had proved hugely popular, but the last one had been held in 2000. The new series was centred around the Metropolitan Railway E class 0-4-4T No. 1 from owner the Buckinghamshire Railway Centre. However, that was still to complete an overhaul, and in the meantime, another steam locomotive was needed for the test runs. In stepped Bill Parker, who agreed to borrow No. 30587 from the Bodmin & Wenford Railway for the purpose. So we ended up with a tank engine built for London overground suburban running now running underground in the capital!

Under a shroud of utmost secrecy, the well tank was delivered to the Underground's Lillie Bridge depot on the Thursday before the test run.

The run also included Metropolitan Railway's electric Bo-Bo No. 12 *Sarah Siddons*, built by Metropolitan Vickers

Two Beattie well tanks reunited on the line they served for 67 years: No. 30587 pilots No. 30585, visiting from the Buckinghamshire Railway Centre, at Bodmin General on September 3, 2010. ROBIN JONES

in 1921, which once worked express services including Pullman trains from Rickmansworth to Baker Street.

Sarah Siddons accompanied No. 30587 on its clandestine trip, connected to the smokebox end of the locomotive, and was used as a passenger accommodation for the 18 guests who had been invited to witness the proceedings, including Peter Hendy, then the Commissioner of Transport for London, Leon Daniels, managing director of Surface Transport and Howard Collins,

the chief operating officer of London Underground.

At the other end of the Beattie, a bogie permanent way wagon was attached, with emergency supplies of Forest of Dean coal in blue sacks and water in giant plastic containers, which could be linked to the engine via a diesel pump if needed.

Going gingerly where no Beattie well tank had ever gone before, the special train left Lillie Bridge just after 1am and first ran to Kensington Olympia, where the platforms were deserted.

Reversing back to Earl's Court and picking up the VIP guests who had been invited on the trip, including the author, the test train then took the District Line through Paddington.

Stopping momentarily at Edgware Road, it then followed the Circle Line route to its destination, Baker Street, a distance of around seven miles.

At Baker Street, the locomotive safety valves opened and blew off while heat and smoke levels in the station were tested. Photography apart, the well tank left proof of brief presence in the form of soot rings on the roof of the tunnel.

The train, with the Beattie providing much of the power despite its sandwich position in the very unorthodox 'permanent way' working, then pulled forward into the tunnel and reversed back to the westbound platform, from which it ran a full power test from Baker Street back to Edgware Road.

Meanwhile two standard tube trains, comprised of S stock and C77 stock, followed the steam train to test the effect, if any, that it had on them.

The train was back in its depot just after 6am, and the test was hailed a resounding success.

Having completed its small hours feat in superb fashion away from the gaze of linesiders, the little Beattie quietly went back to Cornwall by road, leaving other engines to star in the Met 150 celebrations. It had come out on tops, again.

BACK TO ITS BIRTHPLACE

No. 30587 was the subject of a 30742 Charters' photoshoot at the Museum of Science & Industry in Manchester on June 25, 2017. EMMA SEDDON

In June 2017, No. 30587 returned to the city of its birthplace for the first time in 143 years.

No. 30587 was built in Manchester in 1874 as one of 85 constructed by the Gorton firm of Beyer Peacock.

It was displayed for three weeks at the Museum of Science & Industry, based in the Liverpool road terminus of the Liverpool & Manchester Railway.

There, No. 30587 joined the museum's own Robert Stephenson & Hawthorns 0-4-0ST Agecroft No. 1 and replica Liverpool & Manchester Railway 2-2-0 *Planet* to give train rides on the demonstration line.

CORWEN
THE BIG PUSH

Painting by Eric Bottomley
Photos: Dewi Davies and George Jones

LLANGOLLEN RAILWAY PLC STILL HAS £370K OF SHARES AVAILABLE TO PURCHASE. THE REVENUE FROM THESE SHARES WILL GO DIRECTLY TO HELPING US FINISH CORWEN STATION.

OR FURTHER INFORMATION OR TO PURCHASE SHARES PLEASE CONTACT: ADMIN@LLANGOLLEN-RAILWAY.CO.UK OR CALL 01978 860979

CITY OF TRURO:
THE LEGEND THEY TRIED TO HIDE

In 1904, *City of Truro* was recorded running at 100mph with an express train, and is widely regarded as having set an unofficial world speed record. Yet far from cashing on publicity, it would be many years before the Great Western Railway admitted to the feat.

Late Victorian times were boom years for railways. The motor car had still to see commercial production, and an eager public was enthralled by the developments in steam locomotive technology that meant trains could go faster, shrinking Britain and the world at every stage.

The Races to the North, saw the operators of the West Coast Main Line, the London & North Western and the Caledonian railways, compete with the East Coast Main Line companies, the Great Northern, North Eastern and North British railways, to see who could run express services from London to Scotland in the shortest time.

The second set of races, in 1895,

extended the runs to Aberdeen, where both rivals could run into the same terminus, with the routes converging at Kinnaber Junction.

The races regularly made national newspaper headlines and gripped the public imagination. However, they did not last.

Early on Monday, July 13, 1896, the 8pm Down 'Highland Express' from

Euston to Scotland derailed at the Dock Street points to the north of Preston station in the middle of the night.

In an instant, the entire train was ploughing its way along the permanent way, but, thanks to the presence of mind of the drivers, and despite the weight and vast momentum of the train, it was brought to a standstill within a distance of 80yds. Although the engines and the

City of Truro on the turntable in the Great Hall of the National Railway Museum at York on March 6, 2014. ROBIN JONES

Matched with GWR stock, GWR 4-4-0 No. 3440 *City of Truro* passes Sterns on the Severn Valley Railway on October 13, 1985. BRIAN SHARPE

No. 3440 *City of Truro* runs along the coast at Horse Cove near Dawlish in May 2004. It would have taken this route a century earlier, when it set an unofficial 100mph record on Wellington Bank. BRIAN SHARPE

leading coaches were badly damaged, the train stood the tremendous strain remarkably well.

As it happened, it was lightly loaded and only one of its 16 passengers, a young man called Donald Mavor, was killed. Yet the crash sent shockwaves through the rail industry hampering the progress of steam at speed for the next four decades.

The train was hauled by LNWR locomotives No. 2159 *Shark* and No. 275 *Vulcan*, which were easily capable of handling the 200-ton load, but neither driver had driven this particular train before. Furthermore, neither had experience of driving a train non-stop through Preston. A sharp curve at the north end of the station by the goods yard meant that there was a 10mph restriction.

It was later ascertained by Board of Trade accident investigator, Col York, that the express had been travelling around 40-45mph through the station. When it hit the speed restricted curve, instead of going round it, the train effectively carried on in a straight line.

The engines ploughed through the goods yard, with the train coming to rest just short of a bridge wall. Both engines

RIGHT: The Preston accident of 1896 sent shock waves through the rail industry and the resulting public concern over speeding trains ended competition for increasingly fast express services between London and Scotland for nearly four decades. PRESTON DIGITAL ARCHIVE

remained upright but the carriages were scattered across the mangled tracks and one of their occupants was fatally injured.

A subsequent Board of Trade inquiry at Preston heard Col York conclude: "The cause of the accident is clear. A reverse curve without any intervening tangent, without a check rail, with super-elevation suitable only for very low speeds, and badly distributed, and with a radius at one point of only seven chains; a train drawn by two engines each having a rigid wheelbase of 15ft 8in; and lastly a speed of 40mph or more form a combination of circumstances which were almost certain to lead to disaster."

Overnight, public opinion towards 'speeding' trains changed for the worse. There was outright hostility to what was widely seen as placing life and limb at risk for the sake of breaking speed records in pursuit of railway company prestige.

BLANKET BAN ON PUBLICITY

That is not to say that locomotive engineers simply sat back and accepted their lot. Locomotives continued to be run at greater speed, but the concerned public was not told.

In 1899, a series of high-speed test runs took place on the Lancashire & Yorkshire Railway's Liverpool Exchange-Southport line using locomotives from Aspinall's newly introduced 'High Flyer' 4-4-2 class.

It was reported that on July 15, 1899 one such train was formed of Southport-based No. 1392 and five coaches. Timed to leave Liverpool Exchange at 2.51pm, it was recorded as passing milepost 17 in 12.75mins.

That gave a start-to-pass speed of 80mph but, given the permanent 20mph restriction at Bank Hall and the 65mph restriction at Waterloo, the suggestion has since been made that this train attained 100mph.

City of Truro very slowly became a legend after its high-speed feat in 1904. GWT COLLECTION

The L&Y never published details or timings of this test run. It is only because passing times were 'unofficially' noted by local enthusiasts that the 100mph claim is known at all.

In his volume, The Lancashire & Yorkshire Railway, (Ian Allan, 1956), researcher Eric Mason said that such claims in the absence of proper records would be taken "rightly or wrongly, with a large pinch of salt".

Another of the 4-4-2 class, No. 1417 – the test engine for Hughes' back pressure release valves – became enshrouded in "mythical legends" over its performances,

Mason wrote. "Whilst there is no confirmation of an alleged 117mph near Kirkby, there is no doubt whatsoever that the engine did perform some really fast running in the capable hands of driver J Chapman of Newton Heath."

We will never know whether or not Aspinall's locomotive did reach or exceed the magic ton. And the same has to apply to one locomotive, which was to claim an unofficial record of being the first in the world to hit 100mph.

The world at large did not suspect it at the time, but May 9, 1904 was a seminal moment in the history of the

Great Western Railway. It was on that day, on Wellington Bank on the Bristol & Exeter main line that an example of new locomotive superintendent George Jackson Churchward's first design, City class 4-4-0 No 3440 *City of Truro*, became immortalised in legend, if not in undisputable fact.

Observers claimed that it became the first steam locomotive to break the 100mph barrier, reaching 102.3pm while descending the bank with the 'Ocean Mails' special from Plymouth to Paddington. The debate over whether or not it did reach such speeds continues to this day.

City of Truro was one of a class of 20. Ten of them were rebuilt from Churchward's predecessor William Dean's Atbara class engines, the first (No. 3405) being converted in September 1902 and the rest following in 1907-09. The new batch of 10 was built at Swindon in 1903, and included No. 3440.

Driver, Moses Clements, was rostered to take the train, total weight 148 tons comprising a light load of eight-wheeled postal vans with around 1300 large bags of mail on board, to Paddington. The load included bullion as a payment by the Americans to the French for ongoing work on the Panama Canal. By the time the train, had reached the South Devon banks, it appeared that Clements had decided to "go for it".

By the time the locomotive was racing down the gradient from Whiteball Tunnel on the far side of Exeter, it was going faster than any member of the class had gone before.

At around 10.45am *City of Truro* was recorded at 8.8secs between two quarter-

GWR 4-4-0 No. 3440 *City of Truro* pilots GWR small prairie No. 5528 over Pensford Viaduct on April 28, 1957. HUGH BALLANTYNE

mile posts by timer Charles Rous-Marten, who wrote for The Railway Magazine and other journals, and was on the footplate at the time.

This time recorded on the descent of Wellington Bank would correspond to a speed of 102.3 mph; but Rous-Marten's stopwatch read in multiples of ⅕ second, so the next possible longer time it could register was nine seconds, corresponding to exactly 100mph.

Sadly, the driver saw a gang of platelayers standing in their tracks a quarter of a mile away ahead, and braked fiercely while they moved aside, and carried on into Taunton at just 80mph, ruining the recorder's chance to confirm the speed.

Furthermore, there was no secondary timer on board to confirm the claimed speed, so it was never taken as an official record.

Several writers have, over the century that followed, expressed the view that it would have been physically impossible for a 1000hp locomotive such as *City of Truro* to exceed 92mph on that section of line.

THE RELUCTANT LEGEND

A report of a '99-100mph' run appeared in two Plymouth newspapers the following day, after a postal worker on board conducted some unofficial timings with his own stopwatch. However, in those days before the internet, the report by and large went unnoticed by the world's media.

The GWR was initially reluctant to admit to running at such a high speed as it was fully conscious of increasing public concern about superfast trains, the company allowed only the overall timings for the run to be printed; neither The Times report of the following day nor Rous-Marten who at first toed the company line and kept quiet about the 102.3mph claim. His article in The Railway Magazine of June 1904 did not mention the maximum speed. At first, Rous-Martin restricted his reporting of the speed achieved during the event to the minimum of 62mph logged on the ascent of Whiteball summit. He merely described the trip as setting, "the record of records," adding: "It is not desirable at present to publish the actual maximum rate that was reached on this memorable occasion."

At the time, the GWR and the rival London & South Western Railway were locked in a race for the Plymouth to London ocean mails traffic, and while they had not been given permission to do so, some of the Paddington empire's drivers were determined to demonstrate what they and their Swindon-built engines could achieve.

However, neither company had any intention of admitting actions that might have been considered reckless. At the time, the GWR allowed only

Unofficial record-setter No. 3440 *City of Truro* passing through Sydney Gardens in Bath on April 28, 1957. HUGH BALLANTYNE

the overall timings for the run to be published.

It was only in the edition of The Railway Magazine in December 1907 – nearly four years after the event – that the alleged speed of 102.3mph appeared publicly for the first time – and even then it was not attributed to a particular engine.

In the same month as full details were finally published, April 1908, Rous-Marten died from a sudden heart attack. It would be another 14 years before the GWR made much of *City of Truro's* feat, which had showed that a steam train could travel safely at speeds of more than 100mph, and in terms of railway rivalry, placed the Swindon empire at the head of the pack again.

RELEGATION THEN PRESERVATION

As trains became heavier, larger locomotives were needed to pull them.

Churchward's subsequent designs went on to revolutionise the GWR, while

leaving the past behind. While the City class had a 4-4-0 arrangement with four smaller wheels at the front and four larger drive wheels behind, the type was rapidly making way for Churchward's pioneering 4-6-0s.

Another of Churchward's innovations was the move to external cylinders which, as well as providing greater power, also allowed for much more flowing and modern outlines.

City of Truro was rebuilt to a limited extent in 1911, when it was fitted with a superheater and its smokebox was extended. In 1915 it was given piston valves instead of the original slide valves, and was renumbered 3717 in the 1912 renumbering. Members of the City class soon found themselves relegated to secondary duties. All but one member was withdrawn and scrapped between 1927-31. The last in service was City of Truro, which was withdrawn in March 1931. However, a strange twist of fate saw it avoid the cutter's torch.

This GWR icon passed into the hands

City of Truro in British Railways' service at Sutton Scotney on July 17, 1957. GWT COLLECTION

On its first main line run in its second stint in preservation, GWR 4-4-0 No. 3440 *City of Truro* accelerates away from Newport on October 20, 1985. BRIAN SHARPE

City of Truro displayed in the former railway museum at York, which was set up by the LNER. ROBIN JONES COLLECTION

of none other than the London & North Eastern Railway for display in a new railway museum at York.

By the time of its withdrawal, its historical significance was accepted and Churchward's successor, Chief Mechanical Engineer, Charles Collett, requested that the engine be preserved.

GWR's directors had refused to preserve the engine at the company's expense, so it was donated to the LNER's museum, being despatched there from Swindon on March 20, 1931.

An officially verified record of a steam locomotive breaking the 100mph barrier would not be claimed until November 30, 1934, when LNER Pacific No 4472 *Flying Scotsman* accomplished this while travelling between Leeds and King's Cross.

City of Truro was temporarily evacuated from York during the Second World War to a small engine shed at Sprouston in the Scottish borders.

BACK IN TRAFFIC

In 1957, *City of Truro* was removed from the museum in York, overhauled at Swindon and returned to main line service by BR Western Region. It was renumbered to the original 3440, and repainted into the ornate livery it carried at the time of its speed record in 1904, although this was historically incorrect.

Based at Didcot shed, it was used both for hauling excursions as well as timetabled services, usually on the Didcot, Newbury & Southampton line, even spending a few weeks in Scotland, double-heading with other historic preserved engines between Glasgow and Aberdeen in September 1959.

It was withdrawn for a second time in 1961 and was displayed in Swindon's GWR museum from April 15, 1962; renumbered back to 3717 and displayed in authentic plain green livery with black frames. It became part of the newly established National Collection.

GWR 4-4-0 No. 3440 *City of Truro* departs from Scarborough on September 4, 1988. BRIAN SHARPE

A THIRD LEASE OF LIFE

City of Truro was removed from the museum in July 1984, and restored at Bridgnorth on the Severn Valley Railway for the GWR's 150th anniversary celebrations the following year.

City of Truro was a little late joining the celebrations, making its first moves on the railway in early September and heading a main line 'mystery tour to the West Country', which instead ran from Gloucester to Newport on October 20.

It saw further Severn Valley service on special occasions but was based at the National Railway Museum from August 1, 1986 from where it was regularly used on main line outings, sometimes heading 10-coach trains to Scarborough, until the expiry of its boiler certificate after a farewell railtour from Derby to Paddington on May 3, 1992.

In 1990, it revisited its birthplace as part of the National Railway Museum on Tour exhibition in Swindon Works.

No. 3440 was exhibited in the Swindon shopping mall that had been developed by McArthur Glen in part of Isambard Brunel's great locomotive works from

Following its restoration at the Flour Mill workshops, *City of Truro* was based on loan at the Gloucestershire Warwickshire Railway for several years. Here it is seen preparing to leave Toddington on December 3, 2009. ROBIN JONES

1997 but moved back to the NRM in 1999.

For the centenary of its record-breaking run, *City of Truro* was returned to steam yet again at a cost of £130,000, this time in a partnership between the NRM, Bill Parker's Flour Mill workshop at Bream in the Forest of Dean, and Andrew Goodman of the Gloucestershire Warwickshire Railway. Again it was a close-run thing but No. 3440 headed two specials on the Bristol-Kingswear route in May 2004, taking Wellington Bank at a slightly slower speed than in 1904, yet during its brief return to the main line, demonstrating exceptional power for an engine of its size.

Although it headed a few more railtours, including solo runs over the Devon banks, it was decided that main line use was not appropriate for an engine with fairly limited haulage capabilities. However, it saw several years' intensive use, mainly on heritage lines, nominally based at Toddington but visiting nearly all the operational steam lines in the country, large and small.

In 2010 as part of the celebrations to mark the 175th anniversary of the founding of the GWR, *City of Truro* was repainted and took up its authentic No. 3717 guise once again, for the first time while operating in preservation.

However, No. 3717 was withdrawn from traffic at the Bodmin & Wenford Railway in early September 2011 with leaking boiler tubes, and placed on static display at the Locomotion museum at Shildon.

City of Truro runs round its train at Cheltenham Racecourse station on the Gloucestershire Warwickshire Railway on December 3, 2009. ROBIN JONES

GWR 4-4-0 *City of Truro* running as No. 3717 on the Llangollen Railway. LEWIS MADDOX

BELOW: *City of Truro*, repainted in the colours that it carried in latter-day GWR service as No. 3717, at Didcot Railway Centre on May 1, 2010, the open day of the venue's nine-day GWR 175 extravaganza. FRANK DUMBLETON/GWS

THE FINAL STEAMING?

City of Truro briefly returned to service in 2012, and starred in the NRM's Railfest 2012 event, operating on the short running line in the museum yard.

However, it was failed when being prepared to haul steam rides during the February 2013 half-term holidays at the York museum.

A suspected leak was reported during the cleaning of the firebox. The museum's boilersmith investigated, gave the tube a clean and re-expanded it into the tube plate. This action appeared to cure the leak but the boilersmith recommended a low-pressure hydraulic test to ascertain the condition of the tube in question. The workshop team carried out hydraulic testing to 50psi and this confirmed there was a hole in the wall of a tube.

The curatorial and workshop team examined a number of options including a retube to enable the locomotive to be certificated to operate for a further two years, but arrived at the decision that it was in the best interests of the locomotive as a National Collection artefact that it be withdrawn. The decision also took into account the condition of the rest of the boiler and the deterioration of the platework on the tender.

No. 3717 had been booked to appear at events at the Mid Hants Railway, the Gloucestershire Warwickshire Railway and Locomotion at Shildon later in that year.

The NRM's senior curator of railway vehicles Anthony Coulls said at the time: "At present the locomotive is in good

mechanical and cosmetic condition and can be withdrawn and conserved for display with minimal investment. A further two years of operation would certainly result in the need for repainting and additional mechanical work, particularly as the tyres are thin and that additionally its tender tank is in poor condition.

"*City of Truro* has had two good innings in this last period in service from 2004, especially after the repaint in 2010 and most railways who have wanted to operate it on their lines have done so.

"It is a very elderly iconic locomotive and we must remember its place at the heart of the National Collection and our obligation to preserve it for the long-term benefit of the public.

"Therefore, we have agreed that we should withdraw it with dignity now and put together a carefully thought-out conservation management plan to make it ready for public display."

A museum spokeswoman later said: "It is highly unlikely that *City of Truro* will return to steam. As the locomotive is reputed to have been the first to reach 100mph, its place at the heart of the National Collection and as a historic artefact we have an obligation to preserve it for the long-term benefit of the public."

At present, it seems certain that *City of Truro* will steam no more. However, the preservation movement has time and time again proved that nothing is impossible, and therefore it would take a brave man to say "never again" with 100% conviction.

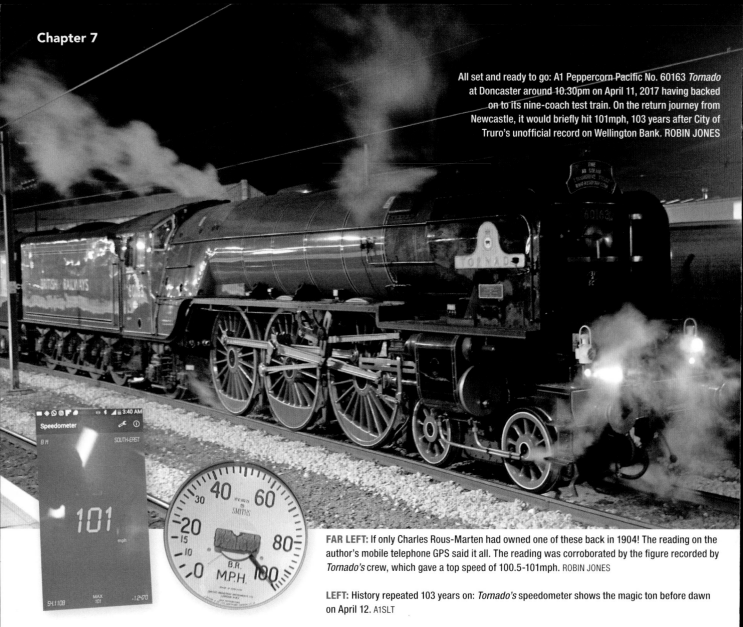

All set and ready to go: A1 Peppercorn Pacific No. 60163 *Tornado* at Doncaster around 10.30pm on April 11, 2017 having backed on to its nine-coach test train. On the return journey from Newcastle, it would briefly hit 101mph, 103 years after City of Truro's unofficial record on Wellington Bank. ROBIN JONES

FAR LEFT: If only Charles Rous-Marten had owned one of these back in 1904! The reading on the author's mobile telephone GPS said it all. The reading was corroborated by the figure recorded by *Tornado's* crew, which gave a top speed of 100.5-101mph. ROBIN JONES

LEFT: History repeated 103 years on: *Tornado's* speedometer shows the magic ton before dawn on April 12. A1SLT

THE ROUS-MARTEN EXPERIENCE 2017

Whether or not *City of Truro* did reach 100mph, its legend is enshrined in history. On April 11, 2017, I trod in the footsteps of Charles Rous-Marten.

I was deeply honoured to have been invited by owner The A1 Steam Locomotive Trust to join a small group of guests aboard the train that was to prove to the world whether new-build £3-million A1 Peppercorn Pacific No. 60163 *Tornado* was capable of regular running at 90mph.

To gain accreditation to run at that speed – the maximum permitted for steam locomotives on Network Rail today is 75mph – *Tornado* would have to show it could better the desired speed by a factor of 10%. And the chance was taken to see if it could run at 100mph.

So it was with great trepidation that I drove to Doncaster station that evening, knowing that history could be made. For until then, no British steam locomotive had reached 100mph in the preservation era.

The outward journey up the East Coast Main Line to Newcastle was made with DB Cargo Class 67 diesel No. 67008 and featured some brisk running well into the 80s, although the train was brought to a shuddering stop at Thirsk when an emergency brake test was carried out. At Tursdale Junction between Darlington and Durham, 91mph was touched, and that was even with the weight of the 67 added to that of the nine largely empty coaches.

The diesel was removed at Newcastle Central, and it was clear that on the return trip, *Tornado* would be going for the big one.

That was achieved in style between Raskelf and Alne south of Thirsk.

I wonder what Rous-Marten would have made of the carriages full of guests studying their mobile telephones and GPS apps to determine their speed?

The accuracy of such devices has often been called into question, especially when compared with locomotive speedometer readings. For instance, when A4 No. 4464 *Bittern* was given special dispensation to run at 90mph with a series of special trains run in conjunction with the Mallard 75 celebrations in 2013, on December 5 that year it hauled the 'Tyne Tees Streak' at what some sources claimed was 94.5mph, itself a preservation-era record.

The train operator afterwards gave an official speed of 93mph, but *Heritage Railway* magazine reader, John Turner, who was in the front passenger coach with his GPS device, recorded 95mph.

Lingering in the back of my mind as we passed Raskelf were the stories of the train crew on *Mallard's* 126mph run down Stoke Bank on July 3, 1938, being offered a taxi alternative if they did not wish to risk life and limb, and damage to the A4's big end.

However, as the magical figures 96, 97, 98, 99 and then 100 flashed up on my GPS device – before it displayed 101mph for a few seconds – the ride was a smooth as any you could wish for on any railway, anywhere.

It appears that my GPS device was not that far out. Both A1 Trust officials on board and the footplate crew confirmed that their own instruments had measured a speed of between 100.5 and 101mph between Raskelf and Alne on the approach to York.

There would be no years of secrecy with this achievement. I was able to jump off the train straight into the comfort of my car, safely parked at Doncaster station, and drive straight to the first available wi-fi hotspot, and before dawn fully broke, broadcast the latest British triumph to a surprised and delighted world, via *Heritage Railway's* facebook.com/heritagerailway page.

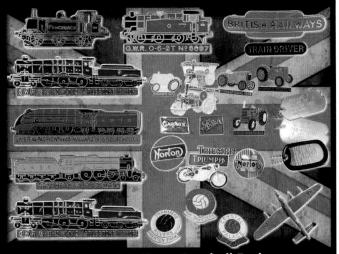

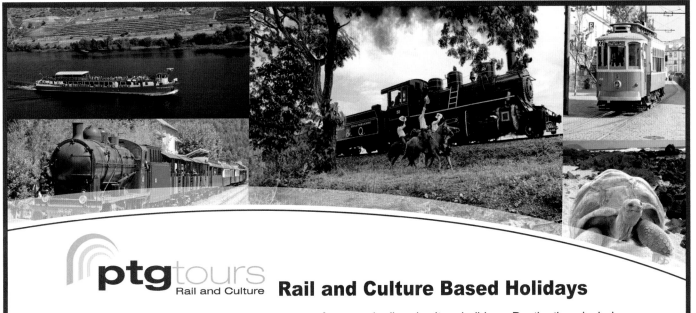

Chapter 8

LODE STAR

Churchward's celestial 4-6-0

A revolutionary evolution of a French design, the Star class blazed a trail for the GWR's 20th-century steam fleet.

GWR Star class No. 4003 *Lode Star* is the oldest surviving four-cylindered GWR express 4-6-0.

In many ways, it highlights a watershed in GWR locomotive design.

After finally converting its last broad gauge lines in 1892, the GWR began a period of modernisation as new cut-off lines shortened its routes to west of England, South Wales and Birmingham. In the Edwardian era, new Chief Mechanical Engineer, George Jackson Churchward, designed or acquired experimental locomotives with different wheel arrangements and boiler designs to help him plan for the future motive power needs of the railway.

Following the success of the prototypes of his two-cylinder Saint class 4-6-0, introduced in 1902, Churchward became interested in developing a more powerful four-cylinder type for the longer non-stop express services.

He persuaded the GWR to acquire three French four-cylinder 4-4-2 compounds for comparison purposes.

In addition Churchward built and tested his own prototype four-cylinder simple-expansion locomotive, No. 40 *North Star* in 1906. Like some early members of the Saint class it was built as a 4-4-2 but designed so that it could easily be converted to a 4-6-0.

In November 1909 it was so converted. The new design incorporated many ideas from the French locomotives including a domeless taper boiler and Belpaire firebox.

The outside cylinders used Stephenson valve gear and drove the second set of driving wheels while the inside cylinders used Walschaerts valve gear and drove the front set of driving wheels. Seven series were built between 1907 and 1923.

In December 1912, *North Star* was renumbered as 4000, and the class became known as the Stars, perpetuating the names of the earlier broad gauge GWR Star Class of 1838.

The first series of 10 locomotives were built at Swindon in 1907 as Lot 168 and numbered 4001-4010.

All except for No. 4010 *Western Star* were built without superheaters. No. 4010 received a Swindon No. 1 superheater and the remainder received superheated boilers between August 1909 and October 1912.

It proved to be a highly successful design in service and 73 Stars were built between 1906 and 1923.

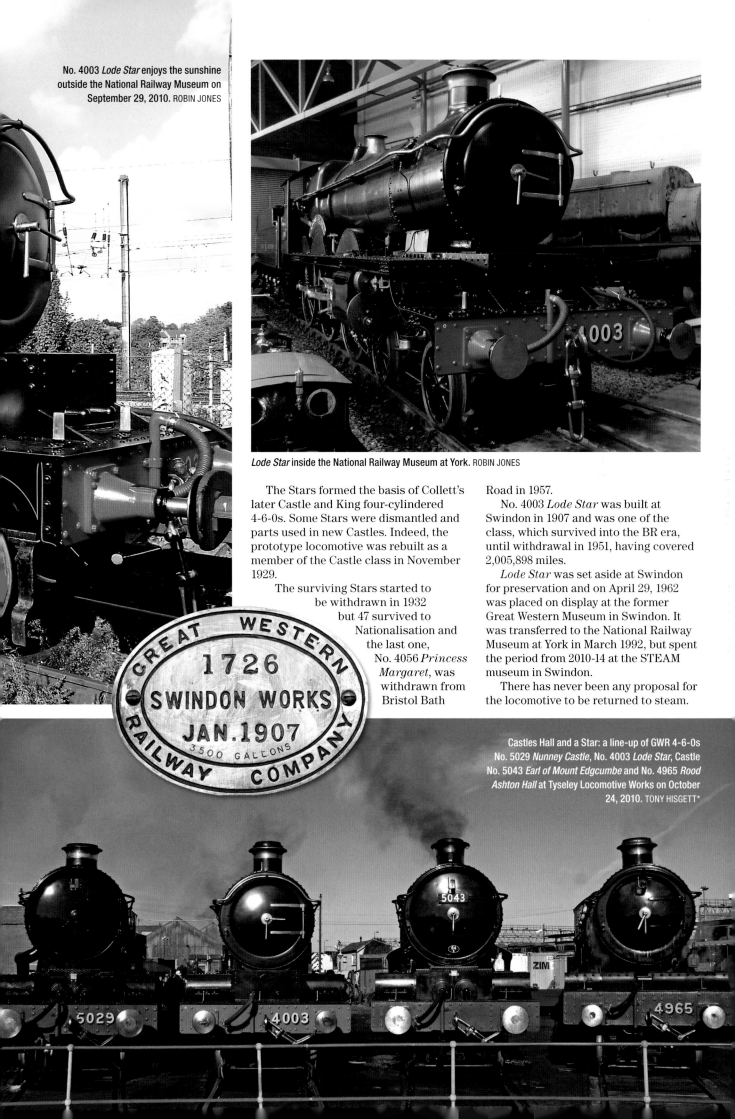

No. 4003 *Lode Star* enjoys the sunshine outside the National Railway Museum on September 29, 2010. ROBIN JONES

Lode Star inside the National Railway Museum at York. ROBIN JONES

The Stars formed the basis of Collett's later Castle and King four-cylindered 4-6-0s. Some Stars were dismantled and parts used in new Castles. Indeed, the prototype locomotive was rebuilt as a member of the Castle class in November 1929.

The surviving Stars started to be withdrawn in 1932 but 47 survived to Nationalisation and the last one, No. 4056 *Princess Margaret*, was withdrawn from Bristol Bath Road in 1957.

No. 4003 *Lode Star* was built at Swindon in 1907 and was one of the class, which survived into the BR era, until withdrawal in 1951, having covered 2,005,898 miles.

Lode Star was set aside at Swindon for preservation and on April 29, 1962 was placed on display at the former Great Western Museum in Swindon. It was transferred to the National Railway Museum at York in March 1992, but spent the period from 2010-14 at the STEAM museum in Swindon.

There has never been any proposal for the locomotive to be returned to steam.

GREAT WESTERN
1726
SWINDON WORKS
JAN.1907
3500 GALLONS
RAILWAY COMPANY

Castles Hall and a Star: a line-up of GWR 4-6-0s No. 5029 *Nunney Castle*, No. 4003 *Lode Star*, Castle No. 5043 *Earl of Mount Edgcumbe* and No. 4965 *Rood Ashton Hall* at Tyseley Locomotive Works on October 24, 2010. TONY HISGETT*

Chapter 9

LSWR T9
No. 30120

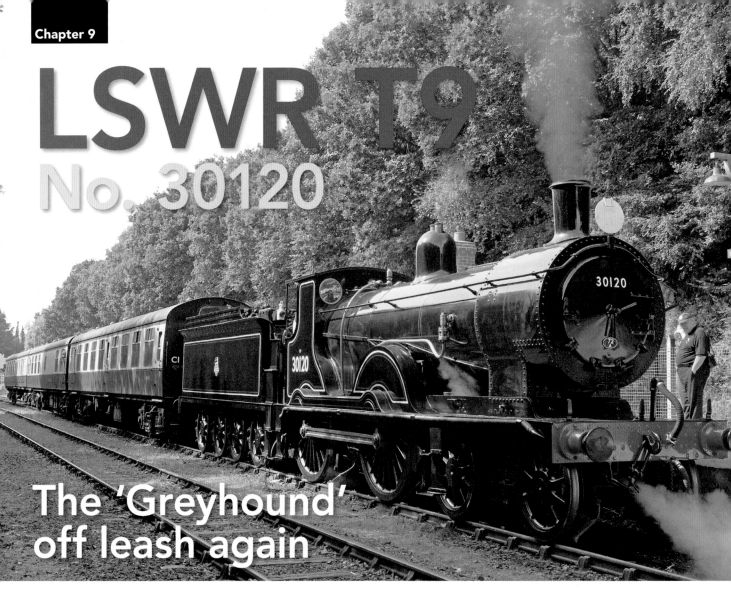

The 'Greyhound' off leash again

Once considered nearly impossible to repair, the sole-surviving LSWR T9 'Greyhound' 4-4-0, No. 30120, was returned to steam on the Bodmin & Wenford Railway, near to where it used to haul the 'Atlantic Coast Express' from Waterloo to Padstow.

It was, of course, not only the operators of the east and west coast routes between London and Scotland that were locked in fierce competition as to which could travel between London and Scotland in the fastest time. The GWR's big rival at the turn of the century was the LSWR, with competing routes between London, Plymouth and the West Country.

LSWR locomotive engineer, Dugald Drummond, designed the T9 4-4-0 for express passenger work over these routes. From 1899, a total of 66 were built and they were nicknamed 'Greyhounds' because of their excellent turn of speed: even in their latter years, they were capable at running at more than 80mph.

They particularly excelled to the west of Salisbury where their light axle loadings and short frame lengths were better suited to the tight curves of the Southern's Western Section.

Construction was shared between the LSWR's Nine Elms Works, which built 35, and Dübs and Company of Glasgow, which built 31, the last of which was exhibited at the Glasgow Exhibition of 1901.

On Drummond's death in 1912, his successor as Chief Mechanical Engineer, Robert Urie, began fitting the class with superheaters.

The T9s were well liked by their crews. LSWR/SR No. 119 (BR 30119) was used by the Southern Railway and early British Railways as a royal engine.

Despite their vintage, 20 still remained in British Railways' service in 1959, but all had been withdrawn by 1963.

One of the class, No. 30120, was designated for preservation as part of the National Collection when it was withdrawn from Exmouth Junction shed in 1961.

However, it was not shunted off to a museum display or storage like other locomotives that had been similarly earmarked. Instead, the Southern Region repaired it at Eastleigh Works from where it was outshopped in LSWR green livery March 1962, to not only work enthusiast specials but also normal services.

It was finally withdrawn from capital stock in July 1963 but continued to work special trains until October of that year.

Following periods in store at Fratton,

Stratford, Preston Park, Tyseley and York, it was overhauled in the early 1980s on the Mid Hants Railway and returned to steam in 1983.

However, because of the steep gradients on the Watercress Line, it moved to the Swanage Railway in 1991 and stayed there until its boiler certificate expired two years later.

Its next move was to the Bluebell Railway, where it remained as a static exhibit on public display and under cover in the engine shed at Sheffield Park, until February 1, 2008. The consensus was that a suspected cracked cylinder block meant that it would never steam again.

In 2007, Helen Ashby, then head of knowledge and collections at the National Railway Museum, asked if *Heritage Railway* could find a permanent home for the T9.

The magazine's staff were delighted to assist.

As we saw earlier, Bill Parker's team at the Flour Mill workshop at Bream had done a stupendous job with the restoration of Beattie well tank No. 30587.

The Flour Mill team had over the year built up substantial specialist knowledge in the field of Victorian locomotives, and when it came to the T9, it was an easy and perfect choice.

Again, retired London banker, Alan Moore, sponsored the overhaul, on the provision that the T9 would be based at Bodmin.

It was delivered to the railway in the summer of 2010 with its classic 4000-galon eight-wheel tender and after undergoing test running, was officially launched into traffic on September 3 that year.

It was an emotional reunion for the locomotive crew, who had both been on the footplate of the same T9 in the early Sixties.

Driver, Gerland Smallcombe, who had been based at Okehampton shed, took No. 30120 from there to Padstow and back in 1961, while his fireman, Tony Hallworth, who had been based at the legendary SR outpost that was Wadebridge shed, remembered driving it for a short distance after it worked a special to Padstow in 1963, following its restoration to LSWR livery.

Helen Ashby, who flagged the T9 off from Bodmin General station, gave a speech in which she praised the Parker-

Restored to LSWR by British Railways in the early Sixties, LSWR T9 4-4-0 No. 120 with Urie stovepipe chimney sits at Tyseley Locomotive Works during a September 1970 open day. HUGH LLEWELYN*

Moore partnership for its achievements in the field of vintage locomotives. The relaunch was followed by a successful four-day gala with four LSWR engines in steam, the two guests being the other surviving Beattie well tank, No. 30585 from the Buckinghamshire Railway

Centre, and M7 0-4-4T No. 53 from the Swanage Railway.

Since then, the T9 has visited other heritage lines, including the Severn Valley Railway and Battlefield Line, with repeat visits to the Mid Hants and Swanage railways.

T9 No. 30120 back on LSWR metals and on loan to the Swanage Railway in the summer of 2016. ANDREW PM WRIGHT

Chapter 10

BUTLER-HENDERSON

Last of the 'Directors'

One of only two surviving locomotives from the original Great Central Railway's locomotive fleet, 'Director' 4-4-0 *Butler-Henderson* steamed for many years on the modern GCR heritage line before becoming a static exhibit.

In 1913, the first of John Robinson's 11E 'Director' 4-4-0s were outshopped for the Great Central Railway.

Highly successful in their own right, four years later Robinson built the 9P 4-6-0 Lord Faringdon class. It was the company's largest passenger locomotive design and the first locomotive was built at the end of 1917 and named after GCR chairman Lord Faringdon. It is said to have been inspired by the LNWR Claughton class, although they had little in common other than they both had four cylinders.

While the 9Ps were better than his previous Class I Sir Sam Fay 4-6-0s, they were not an unqualified success, so five more 4-4-0s were ordered. These new 4-4-0s had a number of modifications and were classified 11F, becoming known as 'Improved Directors'. The most obvious modification was the use of inside admission piston valves. Side cab windows were also installed.

Outshopped between 1919-20, they were allocated to Neasden, to haul expresses as far as Nottingham, and were found to be more successful than the original 'Directors'.

Their 6ft 9in driving wheels made them fast but unsuitable for freight traffic.

A batch of six more were ordered in 1922 and by 1924, the D10s and D11s were working from Neasden and Gorton sheds. From 1927 though, D11s were used on some of the LNER Pullman services out of King's Cross, alternating with GNR C1 Atlantics and allocated to Copley Hill in Leeds.

After Grouping, the LNER needed new express engines for its ex-North British routes in Scotland and opted for a batch of 'Improved Directors', possibly a result of Robinson's continuing influence in the new company. A total of 24, now classified D11s, were built during 1924, modified to fit the lower NBR loading gauge.

While the GCR D11/1s had been named after GCR directors, royalty, and First World War battles the NBR D1/2s continued a theme set by the NBR D30 4-4-0s, and were named after characters in Sir Walter Scott's novels and poems.

By 1938, the D11/1s were allocated to Darnall, Neasden, Gorton and Trafford Park, but 4-6-0s were taking over meaning that the 4-4-0s were rarely seen on first-class expresses. During the early 1950s, D11s were allocated to Trafford Park and Heaton Mersey to operate the Cheshire Lines, but with regional boundary changes, were displaced by LMS types and many were put into store.

The Scottish D1/2s were spread across the NBR system, their duties including express passenger services and special services, as well as the Scottish legs of a number of Pullman services.

They were displaced when the Gresley D49 4-4-0s arrived in Scotland in 1928, but it would not be until the advent of the Thompson B1 4-6-0s after 1945, that the D11s would be completely replaced, and by the 1950s, many of the D11/1s were in storage.

Withdrawals did not start until the end of 1958, with the last of the D11/1s going in December 1960, and the final D1/2 at the beginning of 1962, as diesel multiple units took over operation of the shorter-distance passenger trains,

The first of its class to be built, No. 506, was claimed for the National Collection, representing Robinson's most

GCR 11F or 'Improved Director' 4-4-0s No. 506 *Butler-Henderson*, which was built in 1919, is the sole-surviving GCR passenger locomotive. It is seen on display at Barrow Hill in 2012, and looks set to be an exhibit in the planned new £18-million museum next to the modern Great Central Railway's Leicester North terminus. Capt Eric Brand Butler-Henderson was the seventh child of Alexander Henderson, 1st Baron Faringdon, a soldier and company director, who was honoured when the locomotive was named after him. He is the great-grandfather of Vicki Butler-Henderson, the motoring TV presenter and her brother Charlie Butler-Henderson, a racing instructor and presenter. ROBIN JONES

successful passenger design.

On withdrawal, No. 62660 *Butler-Henderson* was restored to GCR livery as No. 506 and displayed in the British Transport Commission Museum at Clapham. When the museum was closed, it was sent on loan to the modern Great Central Railway, arriving at Loughborough on March 14, 1975.

Indeed, it was the first original GCR locomotive to run there.

Restoration to running order began in 1981. It returned to steam in March 1982 and played a part in regular traffic on the heritage line, but when its boiler certificate expired, it was moved to the National Railway Museum on April 12, 1992.

It is currently on static display at Barrow Hill Roundhouse near Chesterfield, where it was placed on long-term loan in 2005.

Three National Collection locomotives stand around the turntable at Barrow Hill, the last surviving rail-connected roundhouse in Britain. On the far left is Great Eastern Railway Holden G58 (LNER J17) 0-6-0 No. 1217, in its BR livery as No. 65567. It was built at Stratford in 1905 and withdrawn 1962. Next to it are Britain's sole-surviving original Great Central Railway locomotives, O4 2-8-0 No. 63601 and 11F 'Improved Director' No. 506 *Butler-Henderson*. ROBIN JONES

Chapter 11

THE MIDLAND COMPOUND

A stalwart performer in its day that delighted many in the earlier days of preserved main line steam, but Midland Railway compound 4-4-0 No. 1000 has not turned a wheel since 1982.

Midland Railway compound 4-4-0 No. 1000 at the former Steamtown museum at Carnforth. BRIAN SHARPE

In 1875, Richard Deeley became a pupil of Samuel Johnson at Derby Works, eventually replacing Johnson as the Midland Railway's Locomotive Superintendent on January 1, 1904. He progressed with the company's use of compound 4-4-0s started by Johnson but disagreed with the Midland board over its small-engine policy and resigned at the end of 1909.

George Stephenson had built the Midland main lines with shallow gradients, for which smaller engines were adequate for most occasions, and while there were few severe gradients in the Midlands, problems were encountered with the opening of the Settle to Carlisle route.

The small Midland engines were barely, if at all, adequate and double-heading or banking had to be used to prevent stalling.

The company's policy was satirised in a rhyme as follows:

M is for Midland with engines galore
Two on each train and asking for more

A big disadvantage of a small-engines, policy was the reduction of a railway's capacity. More and shorter trains had to be run, while paths had to be created for locomotives running light engine back to base after double-heading or banking duties.

Five 4-4-0s including No. 1000 were built in 1902 by Samuel Johnson, which had a three-cylinder compound arrangement, with one high-pressure cylinder inside the frames, and two low-pressure cylinders outside, utilising Smith's starting arrangement.

From 1905 onwards, Johnson's successor, Deeley, built an enlarged and simplified version, using his own starting arrangement, making the engines

Derby-built Midland Railway compound No. 1000 of 1902. It is now part of the National Collection but has not steamed since 1982. It is pictured inside the Severn Valley Railway's Engine House museum and visitor centre at Highley. ROBIN JONES

simpler to drive. These locomotives were originally numbered 1000-1029, but during the 1907 renumbering scheme the five Smith/Johnson locomotives became Nos. 1000-1004 and the Deeley compounds Nos. 1005-1034, 10 more of these being added in 1908-1909.

They retained their Midland numbers under the LMS, which continued to build slightly modified Compounds, and although of Midland design were extensively used on West Coast Main Line services.

The original Johnson locomotives were all subsequently rebuilt as Deeley compounds, including the now-preserved No. 1000, which was rebuilt with a superheater in 1914.

PRESERVED BEFORE THE NATIONAL COLLECTION

The original compounds were all withdrawn by early BR days. The first, No. 1000, despite being significantly rebuilt, was withdrawn in 1951 but was retained at Derby for preservation, eventually being restored to MR livery in

1914 condition as No. 1000.

It even became one of a very select number of British Railways' preserved engines to be returned to steam, working occasional railtours from 1959 until placed on static display in the Museum of British Transport at Clapham in 1962.

When that museum closed, No. 1000 was moved by rail to the new National Railway Museum at York on April 19, 1975 and returned to steam for the Rail 150 S&D cavalcade at Shildon in August that year.

From April 1976 it was used in occasional railtour service once again, but nearly always double-headed, making two solo runs in private charter trains.

It was loaned to the Dinting Railway Centre at Glossop from October 1978 to May 1979, working both ways from York on tours with LMS Jubilee 4-6-0 No. 5690 *Leander*, and appeared in the Rocket 150 cavalcade at Rainhill in May 1980.

Its finale was a pair of runs over the Settle and Carlisle line in February 1982 in snowy conditions also accompanied by *Jubilee* 4-6-0 No. 5690 *Leander*.

Midland Railway 4-4-0 compound No. 1000 at Derby Works, restored to its crimson lake livery. As British Railways No. 41000, it had been withdrawn back in October 1951 but preserved. BEN BROOKSBANK

It proved the efficiency of the Compound design by using only 1500 gallons of water on this run over the arduous route.

Since then, No. 1000 has been on display at the NMR, the Bo'ness & Kinneil Railway, the Severn Valley Railway Engine House museum and visitor centre and at Barrow Hill Roundhouse, but it has never worked on a heritage line.

Maybe its day will come round again. Let's hope so.

Chapter 12

GREAT CENTRAL O4

The workhorse that helped win the First World War

A classic Great Central Railway design became mass produced for the military during the Great War, and afterwards several of them emigrated for a new life Down Under and elsewhere.

In 1900, one-time GWR apprentice John Robinson joined the Great Central Railway as locomotive and marine superintendent from the Waterford, Limerick & Western Railway.

Robinson designed the 8K heavy freight 2-8-0 with an eye on the new docks being built at Immingham. A superheated version of the earlier 8A 0-8-0, and introduced in 1911, 126 were built before the outbreak of the First World War, and 19 more with larger boilers by the GCR in 1918-21.

Robust, free-steaming and reliable, the Ministry of Munitions chose the design for its own use during the war, encouraged by the GCR general manager, Sir Sam Fay. For use on the Western Front, the Railway Operating Division of the Royal Engineers ordered 521 of the 2-8-0s in 1917-19 to basically the same design as the GCR's 8K.

During the First World War, the 8K was developed into the Class 8M by fitting a larger 5ft 6in boiler, and a total of 19 were built, entering traffic between 1918-1921.

After the war, the surviving ROD locomotives were sold to various railway companies, with the GCR itself buying three in 1919, while the LNWR bought 30 and its Big Four successor the LMS 75. The GWR took 100 of them, and others went to new owners, in Australia and China.

Despite their success on the GCR, many of these had short lives with their new owners, the LMS ones all being scrapped or sold by the Thirties, and half of the GWR fleet gone by 1930, although others survived well into the Fifties.

The last of 13 locomotives sold to the mining firm J&A Brown for use on the Richmond Vale Railway in New South Wales, Australia was not retired until 1973, and three worked in China until 1990.

The LNER inherited 131 8Ks and 17 8Ms, which became LNER O4 and O5 respectively, but all were converted to standard O4s by 1946. These were joined by no fewer than 273 of the former ROD locomotives between 1923 and 1927, bringing the total LNER O4 fleet to 421.

The British government purchased five more LNER O4s from British Railways in 1952 for use at Suez, and they eventually passed to the Egyptian State Railways.

Withdrawals by British Railways began in December 1958. The last examples of the class were withdrawn from Doncaster in April 1966.

THE BRITISH SURVIVOR

Four examples survive. The best-known is No. 63601, which in the late Nineties was restored to run on the modern-day Great Central Railway at Loughborough.

One of the first of the class and originally numbered 102, it emerged from the GCR's Gorton Works in January, 1912. It was renumbered 5102 in June, 1925, 3509 in April, 1946, 3601 in February, 1947 and finally 63601 in September, 1949.

It was allocated to sheds serving the Pennine route from Manchester, through the Woodhead Tunnel, to Sheffield and on to Immingham. Its first allocation was to Gorton on March 14, 1912, and was followed by transfers to Sheffield, Mexborough, Barnsley,

Doncaster, Frodingham near Scunthorpe and Immingham. The locomotive was also involved in the traffic for the development of the steelworks at Frodingham.

Having undergone very few modifications from its original condition, it was withdrawn from service at Frodingham in June, 1963.

As an example of one of the most successful steam locomotive designs ever and one of the final three O4s surviving with a Belpaire boiler, No. 63601 was chosen for preservation in 1960 as part of the National Collection.

With storage space then being in short supply, No. 63601 first went to Doncaster Works, and then Stratford and Brighton. It then moved to Leicester to be housed in a proposed Leicester Museum of Technology at Abbey Meadows Technology Museum.

That project having failed to take off, in 1976 No. 63601 returned to GCR metals in the form of the engine shed at the former Dinting Railway Centre. Locomotive department staff there decided it was restorable, and it was sent to Longsight depot to have its axlebox repaired.

In 1977, Dinting staff said that a completely new tender would be needed because the one fitted to the locomotive was vacuum and not steam braked.

In the end, the restoration carried out there was purely cosmetic. When the centre closed, No. 63601 was sent to the National Railway Museum in York.

By then, there were many in the enthusiast fraternity calling for the O4 to be restored because of its historical importance. The Main Line Steam Trust Ltd was instrumental in bringing it to Loughborough in June 1996. A national appeal to raise the £70,000-plus cost of restoration to full working order was launched, with the trust contributing £2000.

An extensive restoration programme entered its final stages on June 18, 1999, when the retubed boiler passed its steam test before being lowered back into the frames four days later. Unpainted, it was displayed in light steam during the August 7-8 gala that year.

Finally, on January 24, 2000, it moved under its own steam for the first time in 36 years.

Four days later, it was coupled to the line's now-unique Windcutter rake of 16-ton mineral wagons and ran through Swithland Sidings for the benefit of contributors to the national appeal. Its full public debut came the next day at the start of the winter gala weekend.

During the replacement of hundreds of copper boiler side stays in 2001, a new smokebox together with an LNER pattern chimney were fitted.

No. 63061 has also visited other heritage lines including Keighley and Worth Valley and the Churnet Valley railways as well as Barrow Hill. It appeared at the National Railway Museum's Railfest 2012 event in June that year.

Its final run came on June 24, 2012, its last passenger train arriving at Loughborough Central at 5.30pm. By that time it had been based on the heritage-era GCR for 16 years, five more than it had run in traffic for the original company.

After its withdrawal, talks with owner the National Railway Museum began about a second overhaul for another decade on the GCR, or its future use as a static exhibit, maybe in the planned new £18-million museum at Leicester North, alongside other exhibits from the National Collection. The latter seems a more likely course of action.

The three other O4s that survive are all in Australia. Two of them, Nos. 20 and 24 (ROD Nos. 1984 and 2003) are owned by the Dorrigo Steam Railway and Museum Limited in New South Wales.

The third survivor, No. 23, (ROD No. 2004) was initially located at Freeman's Waterhole in New South Wales, as a part of a mining display, but is now at the Richmond Vale Railway Museum.

One of the three Robinson 8Ks surviving in Australia has been cosmetically restored to its First World War condition. In February 1919, GC-built No. 2004 became the 350th ROD locomotive to go to France and was one of 13 bought by the New South Wales mining company of J&A Brown, for which it last ran on June 8. In 1986 it was acquired as a static exhibit at the Richmond Vale Railway and Museum in northern New South Wales, and following two substantial donations, work began in July 2014 to give its worn appearance a facelift. On Saturday, June 10, the Australian Armed Forces Re-enactment Heritage Unit and the 12th Light Horse Brigade Re-enactment Group acted as a guard of honour at a ceremony to unveil it. RVRM

THE NATION'S SECOND BITE

AT THE BIGGEST STEAM CHERRY

When we read reports of crowds trespassing on tracksides just to glimpse *Flying Scotsman*, the world's most famous locomotive, it seems incredible that half a century ago, it came within a whisker of being scrapped because the National Collection did not want it!

Just before the first light of dawn on the morning of April 23, 2017, enthusiasts began amassing around overbridges and other vantage points along the East Coast Main Line north of York, for an event unique in British railway history.

Daylight broke as helicopters circled overhead, as global headlines and newsreel footage were generated at a pace.

Four trains were to run at 25mph from Tollerton into York station. Two of the trains were modern electric sets, another a 40-year-old diesel High Speed Train… and the fourth was… Gresley A3 Pacific No. 60103 *Flying Scotsman.*

Network Rail's works delivery department at Doncaster took possession of all four tracks from Tollerton into York, so two of the trains could run in the 'wrong' direction alongside the other two.

The aim was to promote the forthcoming state-of-the-art trains on the King's Cross to Edinburgh route, the Class 800 Virgin Azuma.

Billed as Virgin Trains' 'Four Trains' event, the spectacle, which was enhanced by unbroken sunshine from a cloudless blue sky, saw the A3 at the head of a set of West Coast Railways' Mk.1s representing the route's illustrious past as it lined up alongside the Class 125 HST and a Class 225 InterCity set, typical of everyday travel on the ECML today, and one of the new Azuma sets.

Each representing one of four generations of ECML motive power, the four trains were amassed in a compound at Tollerton, with *Flying Scotsman's*

train being towed there by one of the A3s' immediate successors, Class 55 Deltic No. 9002 *Royal Scots Grey,* also owned by the National Railway Museum, thereby making up a fifth generation.

Operated by West Coast, *Flying Scotsman's* driver was Ron Smith, with Clive Gould as fireman and Mick Rawling as traction inspector.

The HST set was led by Class 43 power car No. 43238, which in 2015 was renamed *National Railway Museum 40 Years 1975-2015,* to mark the York venue's 40th birthday. The same locomotive previously carried the name *National Railway Museum – The First Ten Years 1975-1985* for 12 years from 1985. An InterCity 125 took the world record for the fastest diesel-powered train, when it was recorded at an absolute maximum speed of 148 mph on the ECML during 1987.

The InterCity 225 electric set was led by Class 82 Driver Vehicle Trailer No. 82205 *Flying Scotsman,* part of the modern-day set continuing the famous named train.

Also a cutting-edge speed machine such as *Flying Scotsman* (official 100mph world record set on Lincolnshire's Stoke Bank in 1934), an InterCity 225 (140mph top service speed) reached 161.7mph – also on Stoke Bank – on September 17, 1989. That set's Class 91 power car, No. 91010, still holds the British locomotive speed record.

The Azuma was the first of the Class 800s built by Hitachi in Newton Aycliffe, County Durham, which is designed to render the Class 125 and 225 sets obsolete, after entering service in 2018.

All four trains ran in a parallel, but staggered, formation to York, after lining up for photographs alongside the Sidings Hotel and Restaurant at Shipton, which was developed on the site of the former Beningborough station.

Speeds kings in their time, the four trains moved off and ran to York at speeds of 20-25mph. No passengers were allowed on board.

At York, Scottish pipers and a brass band welcomed the trains into the platform. Among the waiting guests were Network Rail chairman Sir Peter Hendy and proud NRM director Paul Kirkman.

The event, organised by Virgin Trains, the National Railway Museum, Network Rail, Welcome to Yorkshire and Hitachi, had been nearly a year in the planning stage, after *Flying Scotsman* made its latest comeback in 2016 following a long-running and overdue restoration. The big challenge had been to identity a few hours of time when the tracks would be free to host four trains travelling in the same direction. Tollerton to York, a distance of 10 miles, was chosen partly because engineering works at Thirsk meant that the tracks would be vacant on the day.

NRM assistant curator, Bob Gwynne, said: "The NRM is proud that *Flying Scotsman,* a symbol of engineering excellence, the first steam locomotive to achieve an authenticated speed of 100mph and the first to undertake a non-stop run between King's Cross and Edinburgh Waverley, is taking its place alongside such worthy successors to its speed and style mantle."

Unique in British Railways' history, A3 Pacific No. 60103 took part in a four-train parallel run down to the East Coast Main line to York on April 23, 2017, to promote Virgin Trains' new Azuma sets (second left). The trains represented four generations of East Coast Main Line motive power. Third left was an InterCity 225 electric set led by Class 82 Driver Vehicle Trailer No. 82205 *Flying Scotsman,* while to the far right was a Class 125 High Speed Train. ROBIN JONES

The past and the future of East Coast Main Line trains: *Flying Scotsman* and the first Virgin Trains Class 800 Azuma set at Beningborough on April 23, 2017. ROBIN JONES

Network Rail had taken special care to ensure that there would be no repeat of the trespass incidents that marred *Flying Scotsman's* comeback in early 2016. Staff were despatched to overbridges along the route to ensure that the onlookers remained firmly behind the fences.

At York station, the shining new Azuma stood in its platform for long periods hardly attracting a glance. The crowds had instead massed on the platform next door, where they could get up close to the real star of the show – *Flying Scotsman*. Would there ever be any other?

Not only was *Flying Scotsman* the first steam locomotive in the world to break the 100mph barrier, but it has during its action-packed lifetime been the centre of many other exploits that attracted both national and international attention.

In November 30, 2015, the museum announced the result of a YouGov survey carried out online across four continents, in which participants were asked to name the most famous locomotive and named train. Respondents in the UK, US, India and Australia were asked to name five trains or locomotives they had heard of. And there was a clear winner, *Flying Scotsman*.

The maroon-liveried Hogwarts Express of global Harry Potter fame came in at 25th place, Stephenson's *Rocket* was 14th. The Japanese Bullet train, the only example of which outside of Japan is displayed in the York museum's Great Hall, made it to 10th position. And LNER A4 Pacific No. 4468 *Mallard*, the world's fastest steam locomotive, which hit 126mph on Stoke Bank on the East Coast Main Line in Lincolnshire on July 3, 1938,

made only eighth.

Museum director Paul Kirkman said: "Our survey carried out across four global markets, backs up the claim that *Flying Scotsman* is probably the most famous locomotive and express train service in the world."

Yet back in 1963, this greatest of British transport treasures nearly ceased to exist.

ENTER NIGEL GRESLEY

In 1911, the newly appointed Great Northern Railway Chief Mechanical Engineer, Nigel Gresley, began drawing plans for a locomotive type that would better the route's Ivatt large-boilered Atlantics, and he looked at the American 4-6-2s or Pacifics.

Nobody knows exactly what the origin of the name Pacific was in railway circles. The design was a natural enlargement of the existing Baldwin 4-4-2 or Atlantic type. It had become a convention that new wheel arrangements were named for, or named by, the railroad that first used the type in the USA, in the case of 4-6-2s, the Missouri Pacific Railroad in 1902.

In 1915, Gresley completed plans for a longer version of the Ivatt Atlantic design with four cylinders, but then switched his attention to what he thought was a far better arrangement, that of the Pennsylvania Railroad's K4 Pacific, the first of which had been outshopped the year before. Basically, he took elements of the K4 blueprint to design a modern Pacific.

WHAT'S IN A NAME?

The name *Flying Scotsman* was originally applied to a train rather than a locomotive, and pre-dated the A3 by several decades.

Indeed, No. 4472/60103 was only one of many steam, diesel and electric locomotives that that hauled it.

The express passenger train service running from London to Edinburgh has its origins in 1860; 16 years before Nigel Gresley, who designed the locomotive was born. It was then that the three east-coast companies, the Great Northern, the North Eastern and the North British railways, established the East Coast Joint Stock pool of carriages for through services using common vehicles, so passengers no longer had to change en route between the two capital cities.

Two years later, the first 'Special Scotch Express' ran, with simultaneous departures at 10am from the GNR's King's Cross terminus and the North British Railway's Edinburgh

Waverley. The original journey took 10½ hours, but increasing competition from the rival West Coast route from Euston via Crewe and Carlisle to Glasgow and Edinburgh (run by the London & North Western and the Caledonian railways) and improvements in railway technology saw this time cut to 8½ hours by 1888.

From 1896, the east coast London to Scotland train was modernised, with new features including corridors between carriages, heating, and dining cars. As passengers could now have lunch on the train, the York stop was cut to 15 minutes, but the end-to-end journey time remained 8½ hours.

The train had been unofficially known as the 'Flying Scotsman' since the 1870s, but the year after the Grouping of 1923, the name was was officially adopted by the newly formed London & North Eastern Railway. But the best was not just yet to come, but was already waiting in the wings.

LEFT: Nigel Herbert Gresley (June 19, 1876-April 5, 1941), the Chief Mechanical Engineer of the LNER who designed the company's A1 and A3s, was knighted in the 1936 King's Birthday Honours list.

The first of Nigel Gresley's Pacifics: A1 No. 1470 *Great Northern*, as built. ROBIN JONES COLLECTION

No. 4472 *Flying Scotsman*, then still an A1, departs King's Cross with the 'Flying Scotsman' in 1932. That year, the journey time for the 'Flying Scotsman' train was reduced to seven hours 30 minutes, and by 1938 it had shaved off another 10 minutes. ROBIN JONES COLLECTION

Gresley did not invent the first British Pacific. In 1908, the Great Western Railway's George Jackson Churchward, oversaw the production of No. 111 *The Great Bear*, which was a unique company flagship locomotive that proved a disappointment. Sadly, it did not survive long enough to enter the National Collection. In 1922, Gresley's first pair of A1 Pacifics, Nos. 1470 *Great Northern* and 1471 *Sir Frederick Banbury* appeared. The GNR board was so pleased with them that it commissioned another 10. When the GNR became part of the new LNER at the Grouping only months later, the 10 were being built in Doncaster Works.

The LNER kept Gresley as its CME. He adopted his A1 Pacific design as the standard express passenger locomotive for the LNER main line, and 51 were built between 1923-25, the third of which was GNR No. 1472, (LNER 4472) *Flying Scotsman*, which appeared from Doncaster in February 1923, as serial number 1564.

The locomotive was named after the London to Scotland express, at the same time as it became officially known as the 'Flying Scotsman' and to publicise the train, was displayed at the British Empire Exhibition at Wembley in 1924 and again the following year.

THE NON-STOP SUPERSTAR

Following valve gear modifications, the A1 locomotive's coal consumption was drastically reduced and it was thus found possible to run the service non-stop with a heavy train on one tender full of coal.

That meant the LNER could better the eight hours 15 minutes that had been agreed with the west coast rivals following the end of the last Race to the North.

Ten A1s and their improved successors the A3s (most A1s including No. 4472 were rebuilt into A3s) were designated for use on the 'Flying Scotsman', including No. 4472.

They were each given corridor tenders (with a coal capacity of nine tons instead of eight) to circumvent footplate crew fatigue by enabling a replacement driver and fireman to take over halfway without stopping the train.

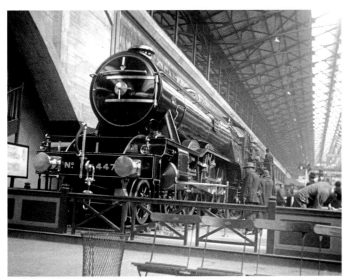

The new train had improved catering and other on-board services, including a barber's shop.

No. 4472 was selected to haul the first of its namesake train's non-stop runs over the 392 miles from King's Cross to Edinburgh on May 1, 1928.

Back then, it was a record time for a scheduled service, but rivals the London Midland & Scottish Railway had stolen

Flying Scotsman fitted with a corridor tender in 1928.

Flying Scotsman heads its namesake train at Craigentinny on July 22, 1932. ROBIN JONES COLLECTION

a march four days earlier, running the 'Royal Scot' non-stop the 399 miles from Euston to Edinburgh as a one-off publicity stunt.

The following year, No. 4472 appeared in the film The Flying Scotsman, enhancing its fame still further.

Flying Scotsman was one of the star exhibits at the now-legendary British Empire Exhibition at Wembley in 1924. NRM

Two Pacifics, different sizes: A1 No. 4472 *Flying Scotsman* alongside Romney Hythe & Dymchurch Railway 15in gauge No. 7 *Typhoon* at King's Cross depot in 1927. Both survive today. ROBIN JONES COLLECTION

THE 100MPH WORLD RECORD

On November 30, 1934, driven by Bill Sparshatt and running a test train down Stoke Bank, *Flying Scotsman* became the first locomotive to be officially recorded as having reached 100mph, and earned a place in the land speed record for railed vehicles.

In doing so, No. 4472 also made not only the fastest long-distance run on any British railway, but probably the fastest journey of its length ever made by steam.

A four-coach train was hauled over the 185.8 miles from King's Cross to Leeds in 152 minutes, and six coaches were worked back in 157 minutes on the same day.

The 250-mile round trip was covered at an average of 80mph, with 40 miles at an average of 90mph, and for a distance of 600yds, the headline-grabbing 100mph.

In the aftermath of the doldrums of the recession of the Thirties, a golden age of luxury and fast travel had dawned on Britain's railways. Unlike the GWR in 1904 when *City of Truro* allegedly reached 100mph, the publicity-conscious LNER was only too happy to make as much as possible out of No. 4472's feat, immortalising the locomotive in the process.

the same year, under an amendment to that plan, it became No. 103. Following Nationalisation on January 1, 1948, *Flying Scotsman* became No. 60103 in December of that year.

THAT GERMAN TOUCH

Under British Railways, A3 Pacifics were subsequently fitted with a double Kylchap chimney to improve performance and economy, but the downside was soft exhaust and smoke drift that tended to obscure the driver's forward vision.

A solution was found in the form of German-type smoke deflectors, which were fitted to the class from 1960, radically changing the A3s' appearance. It is in this form that *Flying Scotsman* emerged from overhaul in 2016.

However, the British Railways Modernisation Plan of 1956 had signalled the end for steam, and its replacement by diesel and electric traction.

The first A3 to be withdrawn was No. 60104 *Solario* in 1959, followed by Nos. 60095 *Flamingo* and 60055 *Woolwinder* in 1961.

In 1962, with other class members still operating on express passenger work, British Railways announced that it would scrap *Flying Scotsman*, and its last scheduled run took place on January 14, 1963. The last A3 to be withdrawn was No. 60052, *Prince Palatine* in January 1966.

Astonishing as it seems to us today, those who drew up the original list for the National Collection did not consider *Flying Scotsman*, or any other A3 for that matter, worthy of saving.

Why not? The locomotive had undergone so many 'Dr Who-style' transformations that while it was a historical entity of great fame, physically it was by no means original. And those choosing locomotives for the collection thought that it was necessary to save only one Gresley Pacific, and that should be an A4, as it was deemed to be the most advanced. So it was decided to wait until record-holder No. 4468 *Mallard* was retired from service and claim that one for the collection.

RIGHT:
Nigel Gresley congratulates the crew of *Flying Scotsman* at the end of its November 30, 1934 trip in which it officially reached 100mph on Stoke Bank in Lincolnshire. NRM

THE FIRST OF MANY 'REBUILDS'

I have often likened *Flying Scotsman* to the science fiction character Dr Who, a member of an alien race which, once he suffers fatal injuries or old age, regenerates into a new body, rather like a caterpillar becoming a butterfly.

History records that the *Flying Scotsman* we see today has undergone so many changes in its career that precious little is left of the locomotive that set that 100mph record, let alone that which emerged new from Doncaster Works. Indeed, it might even be more accurate to describe it as tantamount to a new-build locomotive. No. 4472 ran with its corridor tender between April 1928 and October 1936, after which it reverted to the original type. In July 1938, it was paired

with a streamlined non-corridor tender, and ran with this type until withdrawal.

That in itself was hardly a transformation, but Gresley updated his A1 design to create the A3s. The first appeared on August 22, 1928, and his aim was to convert all A1s into A3s as they entered the works for overhaul.

On January 4, 1947, *Flying Scotsman* was outshopped again from Doncaster Works after conversion to an A3. The major modification included a boiler with the long 'banjo' dome of the type that it carries today.

By this time it had been renumbered twice. Under Gresley's successor Edward Thompson's comprehensive renumbering scheme for the LNER, it became No. 502 in January 1946; in May

Flying Scotsman heads a train comprising LNER Gresley teak coaches. ROBIN JONES COLLECTION

Minus those German smoke deflectors, *Flying Scotsman* waits to depart from King's Cross on April 10, 1961, with the 'Tees-Thames' named train. ROBIN JONES COLLECTION

Flying Scotsman lined up alongside other forms of North American traction at Montreal during its ill-fated transatlantic visit, which bankrupted its saviour Alan Pegler. ROBIN JONES COLLECTION

Flying Scotsman with its two tenders and cowcatchers ready in Darlington for the ill-fated US tour. B MILNES*

STRANDED IN THE USA

In 1969, No. 4472 and a set of Pullman coaches were shipped across the Atlantic to embark on a highly ambitious tour of Canada and the USA, devised by Pegler to promote British goods and services.

Flying Scotsman looked very different as it ran across North America. To comply with local railway regulations it was fitted with a cowcatcher, bell, buckeye couplings, American-style whistle, air brakes, and high-intensity headlamp.

The tour began in Boston, Massachusetts, and ran to New York, Washington and Dallas in 1969, from Texas to Wisconsin and Montreal in 1970, and from Toronto to San Francisco in 1971, a total of 15,400 miles.

Harold Wilson's Labour government's financial support for the tour was withdrawn by Prime Minister Edward Heath's Conservative government in 1970.

Undeterred, Pegler continued running it through 1970, but by the end of that year, the tour had gone broke leaving the locomotive's owner $132,000 in debt.

The A3 ended up in storage at an US army depot at San Francisco docks to keep it out of the reach of angry creditors.

The affair left Pegler bankrupt. He was able to afford the fare home to Britain 1971 only by working his passage on a P&O cruise ship as an on-board entertainer, giving lectures about trains and how steam engines worked.

Again, concern about what would happen to *Flying Scotsman* grew in the UK. It had escaped the scrapyard once: could it face a similar fate again, or be forever lost to its homeland?

In stepped multi-millionaire enthusiast William McAlpine, a director of the construction company Sir Robert McAlpine.

He bought it for £25,000 direct from the finance company in the docks and returned it to Britain.

McAlpine paid for it to be restored in Derby Works, and in the summer of 1973 ran it on the Paignton & Dartmouth Steam Railway.

No. 4472 was then relocated to the Steamtown museum at Carnforth, back then a popular bolthole for preservation, which became its base for a series of main line tours.

In December 1977, *Flying Scotsman* entered the Vickers Engineering Works in Barrow-in-Furness for heavy repairs, including the fitting of an unused replacement boiler.

SAVED FROM THE SCRAPYARD

A group called Save Our Scotsman hurriedly drew up plans to buy No. 4472, but in those early days of railway preservation, were unable to raise the £3000 asking price, the scrap value of the locomotive.

A saviour was to appear in the form of one of the leading lights of early railway preservation. History records that the first volunteer-led takeover of a railway was that of the Talyllyn Railway in 1951, but around the same time, revivalists were looking at the moribund Ffestiniog Railway, a slate-carrying line in Snowdonia.

Businessman and enthusiast, Alan Pegler, who had first seen *Flying Scotsman* at the Wembley exhibition in 1924 saved the Ffestiniog Railway in 1954, setting in motion a chain of events that would turn the line into one of the top narrow gauge tourist railways in the world.

In 1961, Pegler received £70,000 for his shareholding when Northern Rubber was sold to Pegler's Valves, a company started by his grandfather.

With spare cash on his hands, he stepped in and bought *Flying Scotsman*

LEFT: Ffestiniog Railway saviour and businessman, Alan Pegler, stands on the front of *Flying Scotsman* at King's Cross in 1963 after buying it from British Railways to save it from the scrapyard. NRM

outright from British Railways. It is purely thanks to him, not the originators of the National Collection, that this wonderful crowd-pulling celebrity machine can be enjoyed by so many people today.

Pegler ploughed much of his money into having the locomotive restored at its Doncaster Works birthplace, to as close as possible to its LNER condition, in that company's livery.

The German-style smoke deflectors were removed, the double chimney was replaced by a single chimney, and once again No. 4472 – to which *Flying Scotsman* reverted – was paired with a corridor tender.

He then convinced the British Railways' board to allow him to use *Flying Scotsman* on enthusiasts' specials, including in May 1968 for the 40th anniversary run of its non-stop London to Edinburgh feat.

Modernisation saw facilities for serving steam locomotives being ripped out all over the system, so in 1966 Pegler bought a second corridor tender for use as an extra water carrier. Indeed, after British Rail imposed a ban on steam haulage after the legendary '15 Guinea Special' on August 11, 1968, No. 4472 was the only steam locomotive permitted to run on the national network.

Flying Scotsman Down Under in 1989, when it was equipped with electric lighting and air brakes for operation on Australian railways. ROBIN JONES COLLECTION

WOWING THE CROWDS DOWN UNDER

Flying Scotsman's globetrotting days were far from over, despite the experience of the ill-fated North American tour.

It was booked to take part in Australia's bicentennial celebrations in 1988, in place of the requested *Mallard*, 50 years after the A4's world steam record run.

Instead it was No. 4472 that became a centrepiece of the Aus Steam '88 event that October.

It also headed a series of railtours including a return transcontinental run from Sydney via Alice Springs. In doing so, it became the first steam locomotive to travel on the new Central Australia Railway.

THE PEOPLE'S ENGINE SECOND TIME ROUND

Flying Scotsman was owned by a consortium, which included McAlpine, by then Sir William McAlpine, and pop mogul Pete Waterman, himself a former British Railways worker and railway enthusiast in his own right.

Sadly, by 1995, No. 4472 was in pieces in Southall depot, without the necessary finance to return it to main line condition.

The following year, the late pharmaceuticals entrepreneur Dr Tony Marchington came to the rescue, bought it and over the next three year, spent £1 million on restoring it under the helm of engineer Roland Kennington.

In 1999, it made several clandestine test runs in grey primer livery, before it was repainted in LNER apple green livery.

Running in the first few months of the Marchington regime without the smoke deflectors, its comeback run on July 4, 1999, drew massive crowds alongside the East Coast Main Line to as it ran from King's Cross to York.

Marchington drew up plans for a Flying Scotsman Village, firstly at a site near Ambergate in Derbyshire and then in Edinburgh, and Flying Scotsman plc was floated on the junior stock exchange OFEX.

However, Edinburgh City

Council rejected the plans, and in September 2003, Marchington was declared bankrupt. In October 2003, the company announced losses of £474,619, and said it did not have sufficient finance to trade after April 2004, leading to suspension of its shares.

Heritage Railway magazine subsequently discovered that *Flying Scotsman* was being quietly offered for sale through a luxury second-hand car dealership.

In February 2004, a debt agency acting on behalf of Flying Scotsman plc announced a sealed-bid auction for the locomotive in early April.

Again, fears were raised that the world's most famous locomotive might be sold abroad, never to return.

On behalf of the National Collection, the National Railway Museum successfully bid £2.31 million, the money coming from a nationwide public appeal; a £1.8 million grant from the National Heritage Memorial Fund; £70,000 raised by the Yorkshire Post and Virgin Trains' founder Richard Branson matching the £350,000 in public donations.

The sale included the spare A3 boiler used by No. 4472 from 1965-78, the one

on the locomotive as sold being from an A4.

At last, the colossal mistake made by the National Collection in 1963 was rectified. The nation's favourite locomotive was at last owned by the nation.

Serenaded by pipers, *Flying Scotsman* made a triumphant entry into York to open the museum's hugely successful Railfest 2004 event, which marked 200 years since Cornish mining engineer, Richard Trevithick, gave the first public demonstration of a steam locomotive.

Afterwards, it re-entered service on the main line, hauling charter trips, including the 'Scarborough Spa Express'. However, its poor mechanical condition resulted in several failures and heavy repair bills.

It last steamed on December 20, 2005, after hauling a series of Christmas dining trips from Tyseley Locomotive works in Birmingham.

The National Railway Museum then set about overhauling the A3 in its York workshops, with the aim of returning *Flying Scotsman* to its original specification. It was estimated that the overhaul would take a year and cost £750,000, but the museum was proved wrong on both counts.

LEFT: Following its £1-million rebuild under Dr Tony Marchington, *Flying Scotsman* prepares to depart King's Cross with its comeback run on July 4, 1999. ROBIN JONES

RIGHT: Alan Pegler interviewed for TV alongside *Flying Scotsman* at the opening of the Railfest 2004 event at the National Railway Museum. ROBIN JONES

In Perth it was reunited with GWR 4-6-0 No. 4079 *Pendennis Castle*, which had stood alongside *Flying Scotsman* at the Wembley exhibition of 1924, and had been sold by William McAlpine to an Australian mining company. (In 2000, Pendennis Castle returned to Britain and passed into the ownership of the Great Western Society at Didcot Railway Centre, where at the time of writing in 2017, it is being overhauled.)

On August 8, 1989, *Flying Scotsman* set another record en route to Alice Springs from Melbourne, when it ran from Parkes to Broken Hill non-stop, the longest such run by a steam locomotive ever recorded.

That tour also saw No. 4472 better its own haulage record, heading a 735-ton train over the 490 miles between Tarcoola and Alice Springs.

This time round, there was no threat of the A3 being stranded abroad, as the tour had been financed properly, and it was shipped back to the UK in 1990.

Its main line ticket expired in 1993, leaving it to run on heritage railways.

Another regeneration saw *Flying Scotsman* return to its British Railways' guise with the refitting of the German smoke deflectors and double chimney, and repainted in Brunswick green livery.

SPEAKING TOO SOON

The A4 boiler that had been carried by *Flying Scotsman* its its previous running days was sold by the museum, which instead decided, for the sake of historical authenticity, to repair the spare A3 one, which was sent to Ian Riley's workshops at Bury.

However, issues arose with the boiler restoration pushing back the completion date, and then other major problems including misaligned frames and a cracked right-hand cylinder were discovered.

A further public appeal was launched in a bid to raise £250,000 towards the repairs.

It was decided that *Flying Scotsman* should at first appear in its former wartime black livery as NE No. 502. As such, it was ceremoniously unveiled to the waiting world at the museum on the evening of May 27, 2011.

It was by no means all that it seemed. Within weeks, further defects were discovered, including numerous latent cracks throughout the frame assembly as well as cracks in the horn blocks. The main stretcher bar, horn ties and middle cylinder motion bracket were found to be beyond repair and new replacements were ordered.

An independent report was commissioned, which said that the museum had vastly underestimated the work required owing to the poor condition of the A3, partly because of a rushed inspection.

In October 2013, the museum

The official relaunch of *Flying Scotsman*, still in black livery, on the turntable in the Great Hall of the National Railway Museum on the evening of May 27, 2011. However, the jubilation was short lived, as days afterwards, serious problems with the locomotive were discovered. ROBIN JONES

Back on the main line after 11 years: coupled to a diesel, *Flying Scotsman* enters Bury (Bolton Street) station on January 6, 2016. ROBIN JONES

Flying Scotsman departs from a packed Bury (Bolton Street) station on the East Lancashire Railway, on January 8, 2016, hauling its first public trains since overhaul. ROBIN JONES

announced that Ian Riley had successfully tendered to complete the restoration, in return for being allowed to operate it for the first two years.

It was subsequently decided for historical accuracy to return the locomotive to service in the form that it was withdrawn in 1963, numbered 60103, with double chimney, smoke deflectors and Brunswick green livery, a first choice for enthusiasts who remembered the A3s in action in latter British Railways days.

Flying Scotsman finally emerged from Ian Riley's Baron Street works in Bury, after dark on the evening on January 6, 2016, and, coupled to a Class 31, diesel ran to Bury (Bolton Street) station on the adjoining East Lancashire Railway.

For the next two weekends, when it hauled public trips on the heritage line as part of running-in-tests, seats on the train sold out quickly as around 20,000 people flocked to the Irwell Valley to see it back in action.

Still in black livery, its first main line run was the Railway Touring Company's 'Winter Cumbrian Mountain Express' from Carnforth to Carlisle on February 6. However, a hot bearing and spring needed attention, followed by the discovery of a cracked driving wheel spring.

The leading pair of driving wheels were removed and sent to Bury where the bearings were examined and the problem rectified.

The wheels were refitted on February 19 and a test run from York to Scarborough completed on February 23. No. 60103, and a support coach ran down the East Coast Main Line to London on February 24, in time for its official comeback run from King's Cross to York the following day.

As crowds pack the platforms to glimpse the world's most famous locomotive, *Flying Scotsman* departs from King's Cross with its official comeback trip on February 25, 2016. VIRGIN TRAINS EAST COAST

ALL'S WELL THAT ENDS WELL, BUT...

Friday, February 25, 2016, saw *Flying Scotsman* haul its 11-coach comeback train out of King's Cross at 7.40am.

Crowds not only gathered at the station and along the route, but on the track itself. At points near St Neots and north of Doncaster, the locomotive was brought to a stop because of trespassers eager to get the closest view possible of No. 60103. For some, it seemed, its celebrity status overrode any thoughts of health and safety.

Trespass would become a big issue for the operator of the locomotive in the months that followed. When a planned trip through East Anglia was cancelled because of fears of trespass, it appeared that the locomotive, which back in 1963 so nearly ended up as packs of razor blades, was now too famous to run.

However, the cost of £4.5 million to overhaul the locomotive, a figure released by the museum in September 2016, over and above the £2.31 million purchase price not only made *Flying Scotsman* the most famous locomotive in the world, but also the most expensive.

However, all thoughts of the costly mistakes that had been made in the long-running overhaul quickly evaporated as far as a delighted and enthusiastic general public was concerned, as the big green machine roared back on the main line, with, it seems, more people taking it to their hearts than ever before.

A total of 297 VIPs, fundraisers, competition winners and members of the public, who paid up to £450 each, were on board the relaunch trip. Among the VIP guests was Ron Kennedy, 83, who began his career as a teenage cleaner at King's Cross and who drove *Flying Scotsman* from 1956 until it was sold to Alan Pegler in 1963, Davina Pike, Pegler's

Flying Scotsman stands in Platform 9 at York on February 25, 2016, after arriving 53 minutes late from King's Cross because of two major trespass incidents. ROBIN JONES

personal assistant on the tour of North America in 1969-70, and former owner Sir William McAlpine and his wife Judy. "It's a wonderful locomotive like a beautiful woman," he said. "She's in the right place doing the right thing and very much loved by everybody, and the wonderful thing about her, she makes people smile, people love her."

On the downhill stretch past Biggleswade, Sandy and Tempsford, the A3 averaged 75.13mph over the 12 miles between Mileposts 38 and 50, and crowds were there at every station platform, overbridge and lineside vantage point, to wave and cheer the train, while five helicopters followed it to gather news footage.

At York, Platforms 9 and 10 were heaving with spectators for up to two hours before the train finally arrived, 53 minutes late because of the trespass

The cabside numerals being applied inside the National Railway Museum's workshops on January 17, 2016, after staff from Heritage Painting repainted the locomotive from wartime black into the Brunswick green livery that it carried in British Railways days. ROBIN JONES

problems. Station and NRM staff handed out special *Flying Scotsman* flags and sweets.

Uncoupled from its train *Flying Scotsman* steamed into the museum's north yard, for a final welcome-home ceremony and speeches to mark the start of Scotsman season.

Museum director, Paul Kirkman, said: "We have all been looking forward to the day when *Flying Scotsman* steams home to York along the East Coast Main line and now this historic moment has finally come to pass. This celebratory journey marks a new stage in this steam icon's long and colourful history, and is a tribute to all the people who have worked so hard to make this happen, from those that have worked on the restoration itself to the public that donated to our appeal to bring this legend back to life."

Yet what was the true nature of the beast that was now the subject of worldwide adoration?

As stated above, at every overhaul, plus the upgrading from an A1 to an A3, parts big and small were changed. All that is left of the original 1922-23 locomotive that did 100mph in 1934 is the rear two thirds of the frames, part of the cab sides, some parts of the motion and possibly the driving wheel splashers.

Tradition holds that the frames of a locomotive give it an identity, and change as many other parts as you like, it will still be the locomotive as built. Yet in reality, the *Flying Scotsman* of today is more an historical entity than a physical artefact in its own right. Compare and contrast with BR Standard 9F 2-10-0 No. 92220 *Evening Star*, which museum staff will tell you is the most complete original steam locomotive in the National Collection.

An analogy is home computing: you buy a PC from a store, and as computer technology advances with every passing year, you might upgrade a component. Add more RAM, buy a bigger screen, replace your wired mouse with a wireless one, buy an extra or bigger hard drive, maybe replace the motherboard or graphics card and at some time the case itself. What you have left is a direct descendant of your original purchase, but it is not the same.

If you have supported a football team for 20 years, how many of the team from the first game you watched are still playing two decades later? Yet it is exactly the same club!

Here, as far as an eager public is concerned, *Flying Scotsman* remains a definitive icon of the steam era, an age in which Britain led the world in so many respects, including transport technology.

And what about the famous train from which the locomotive took its name?

Of course, it was not only No. 4472 that hauled 'Flying Scotsman'. Several A1s, A3s and A4s took their turn.

From October 6, 1958, diesel haulage of the train began, at first by Class 40s,

and in 1962 Class 55 Deltics took over.

Under British Railways, the 'Flying Scotsman' ceased to be a non-stop train, calling at Newcastle, York and Peterborough.

Following privatisation, successive ECML operators including Virgin Trains East Coast, the current franchise holder, have retained the named train.

On May 23, 2011, the 'Flying

Scotsman' brand was relaunched for a special daily fast service comprising an electric InterCity 225 set and operated by East Coast departing Edinburgh at 5.40am and reaching London in exactly four hours. In October 2015, Class 91 power car No. 91101 and trailer No. 82205 were revinyled in a new *Flying Scotsman* livery and relaunched by Scotland's First Minister Nicola Sturgeon.

Flying Scotsman lets off steam preparing for departure to York as it stands alongside a Virgin Trains electric Intercity 225 set at King's Cross on February 25, 2016. VIRGIN TRAINS EAST COAST

LEFT: Penny Vaudoyer, daughter of *Flying Scotsman* saviour Alan Pegler, as well as Sir William McAlpine, who rescued the A3 from California, welcome the restored locomotive to the National Railway Museum on February 25. Alan Pegler died on March 18, 2012, aged 91. ROBIN JONES

Flying Scotsman comes face to face with its modern-day electric namesake at the National Railway Museum on March 26, 2016. PAUL BICKERDYKE

Flying Scotsman passes Ais Gill with the Oxenhope-Carlisle trip on March 31, 2017, which reopened the Settle and Carlisle route. BRIAN SHARPE

FLYING SCOTSMAN REOPENS THE SETTLE AND CARLISLE LINE

Flying Scotsman launched its 2017 programme by reopening the Settle and Carlisle route by hauling a sell-out excursion from Oxenhope on the Keighley & Worth Valley Railway, thereby adding yet another chapter to its illustrious history.

The legendary trans-Pennine route had been closed north of Armathwaite since February 9, 2016 after a serious landslip at Eden Brows. Network Rail's engineers and contactors spent 14 months rebuilding and stabilising the trackbed in time for the line to be reopened to through traffic on March 31.

The work had involved clearing the 70-metre slope of vegetation and excavating four metres below track level before installing piles. A total of 16,000 tons of spoil had to be removed from the site before a concrete guide wall could be installed to assist with piling works using 226 steel-cased piles, followed by pouring in 1300cu m of concrete.

Flying Scotsman travelled with its support coach from the National Railway Museum to the KWVR on Wednesday March 29, ready for the excursion to Carlisle, which was followed by a week's operation on the KWVR.

Departing from Oxenhope at 8.30am, with a 10-coach train of maroon Mk.1 stock from West Coast Railways at Carnforth, Scotsman joined the Aire Valley main line at Keighley to head for a water stop at Hellifield.

After an on-time departure, the special topped the climb to Blea Moor eight minutes early, continuing to Appleby where it was greeted by a piper and speeches were made to mark the occasion.

After Appleby, the train crossed the newly reinstated section of track at Eden Brows with much whistling and was watched by the large team of engineers who had carried out the work of rebuilding the line.

The engine was turned and serviced at Carlisle before retracing its steps to Keighley, from where a banking engine was required over the 1-in-58 gradients of the Worth Valley branch. All seats on the train at £220 per ticket were sold many weeks in advance and the event made headlines nationally, although the BBC was criticised for using old footage of *Tornado* on Ribblehead viaduct instead of *Flying Scotsman* on the day!

AND STILL THEY COME...

Incidents of trespass, which had caused problems for the train operator and British Transport Police during 2016, began to diminish as the novelty factor of seeing the A3 back in action faded.

However, the problem has not gone away. On May 19, 2017, Steam Dreams' 'Cathedrals Express' from Newport to Gloucester and back via Bristol Parkway was marred by trespassing incidents as spectators risked a £1000 find to get a closer view of the legendary locomotive as it passed through Gloucestershire.

No. 60103 departed Gloucester late because trespassers had climbed fences further down the line.

As hundreds of spectators waited at Cam & Dursley station, where the car

LEFT: Although its speed was limited to 25mph for Virgin Trains' Four Trains quadruple running event on April 23, 2017, *Flying Scotsman* looked every bit the part with a spirited departure from Beningbrough for the short trip to York. ROBIN JONES

Flying Scotsman seems to have the uncanny knack of making railway history at every twist and turn. During its April 2017 visit to the Bluebell Railway, Liz Groome, daughter of former Nine Elms driver, Clive Groome, who for many years offered steam driving courses through his Footplate Days and Ways outfit, drove the A3, with her sisters Ruth and Rebecca acting as fireman and cleaner. The turns were conjectured to be the first time that No. 60103 had been operated by an all-female crew, and formed a direct link with the end of Southern steam 50 years before, when their dad worked for BR. ANDREW OLDHAM

During *Flying Scotsman's* visit to the Bluebell Railway in spring 2017, the Romney, Hythe & Dymchurch Railway took the opportunity, with help from the A3's former owner, Sir William McAlpine, to reunite it with Pacific No. 7 *Typhoon* at Sheffield Park. The meeting, recreated the famous one between the pair at King's Cross shed in 1927. In a 'Scotsman through the gauges' special display, a third Gresley-inspired Pacific – a 10¼in gauge version of No. 4472 *Flying Scotsman* – attended from the South Downs Light Railway at Pulborough, while in the locomotive shed were a collection of A1/A3s in miniature. TONY PAGE

park was packed and cars vied for space on grass verges, the trip was halted for half an hour at Standish while two police officers walked up the line, calling to the trespassers to move back behind fences.

Three people were spotted only a few yards from the track at Cam & Dursley, while around 400yds up the line, police spoke to more people.

Following these incidents, Steam Dreams decided to stop publishing timings of *Flying Scotsman*-hauled trains on its website in advance.

In 2016, No. 60103 showed its ability to pull crowds as well as trains with hugely successful visits to the Tyseley Locomotive works, the East Lancashire, North Yorkshire Moors and Severn Valley railways, at the latter taking part in a Pacific Power event with new-build *Tornado*, a locomotive that some observers see as being to 21st-century steam what *Flying Scotsman* was to the 20th.

High-profile visits to the Keighley & Worth Valley, Bluebell and West Somerset railways and Didcot Railway Centre followed in 2017.

Although the Four Trains event on the East Coast Main Line on April 23, 2017 took place at dawn, *Flying Scotsman* remained on display at York station until mid-morning, by which time a sizeable crowd had gathered. ROBIN JONES

Ringing the changes 44 years apart: *Flying Scotsman* in LNER livery with no German smoke deflectors passes Culham with a Locomotive Club of Great Britain 'Cathedrals Express' special from Didcot to Tyseley in September 1973, and the same spot on June 13, 2017, in Brunswick green livery with the smoke deflectors, hauling a Steam Dreams' 'Cathedrals Express'. KEN MUMFORD

Saved for the nation, but for long left forgotten and forlorn, music producer Pete Waterman came to the rescue of LNWR eight-coupled 'Super D' No. 49395 and returned it to steam at great expense.

LNWR 'Super D' 0-8-0 No. 49396 passes Quorn & Woodhouse on the Great Central Railway with a goods train in February 2005. BRIAN SHARPE

The London & North Western Railway built the first eight-coupled freight engine intended for service in Britain in 1892, although the much smaller Barry Railway had earlier bought a number of second-hand 0-8-0s originally destined for Scandinavia.

By 1922 the LNWR had the largest fleet of 0-8-0s in the country, having ceased to build 0-6-0s as early as 1902.

They were the workhorse of the railway's coal and heavy goods traffic for many years, continuing through LMS days, and right up to withdrawal of the last four from Bescot shed in 1964.

LNWR Chief Mechanical Engineer Francis Webb's successor, George Whale, was appointed in April 1903 and is credited with the development of Webb's Precedent 2-4-0 into the Precursor 4-4-0 and the beginning of the somewhat confusing conversion of the many varieties of LNWR heavy freight 0-8-0s into what eventually became known as the G2 class.

Webb had built 282 0-8-0s but all apart from the first one were compounds, of which 111 had two high-pressure cylinders outside the frames and one low-pressure cylinder inside, known as Class As from 1911, while there were 170 Class B engines, which had two inside low-pressure cylinders.

Under Whale, 36 Class Bs became 2-8-0s but remained as compounds. Twenty six retained their original boilers and were later designated Class E, but 10 of those converted from May 1906 were provided with larger boilers and were later designated Class F.

The Class As were rebuilt as four-cylindered simple 0-8-0s with their original boilers, and designated Class C, but 62 Class As were given larger boilers and became Class D. The last 34 conversions from Class A to simples with original boilers became Class C1 as their new cylinders were a different size.

The Class Bs were then rebuilt as 0-8-0 two-cylindered simples with the larger boiler to become Class G with 60 new Class Gs built in 1910. The first of the Class Gs were fitted with superheating and became Class G1 in 1912. The LMS inherited the other 91 in 1923 but rebuilt them all to Class G1 between 1924 and 1937.

A further 170 Class G1s were built between 1912 and 1918.

Under CME Hewitt Beames, the LNWR built 60 G2 0-8-0s with higher pressure boilers in 1921-22. Uniquely among the LNWR 0-8-0s, these were never rebuilt from or into other classes.

The G2, together with a relatively short-lived 0-8-4T version were the last locomotives to be built anywhere with Joy valve gear, which worked off the movement of the connecting rods, rather than from eccentrics, and resulted in a distinctive 'wheezing' exhaust sound.

Both the LNW and Lancashire & Yorkshire railways persisted with this gear to the end of their existences, but it was rarely employed elsewhere after 1900.

No. 485 was the prototype of this final G2 design. The LNWR built 40 of them at Crewe, originally fitted with boilers supplied by the North British Locomotive Company in Glasgow. Very soon, all were rebuilt with Belpaire boilers, and that carried by No. 485 was one of the final batch of 10 built at Crewe in 1944.

When the LNWR merged with the Lancashire & Yorkshire Railway in 1922, it was George Hughes from the L&Y who became the first CME of the LMS.

Most of the G1s and G2s were fitted

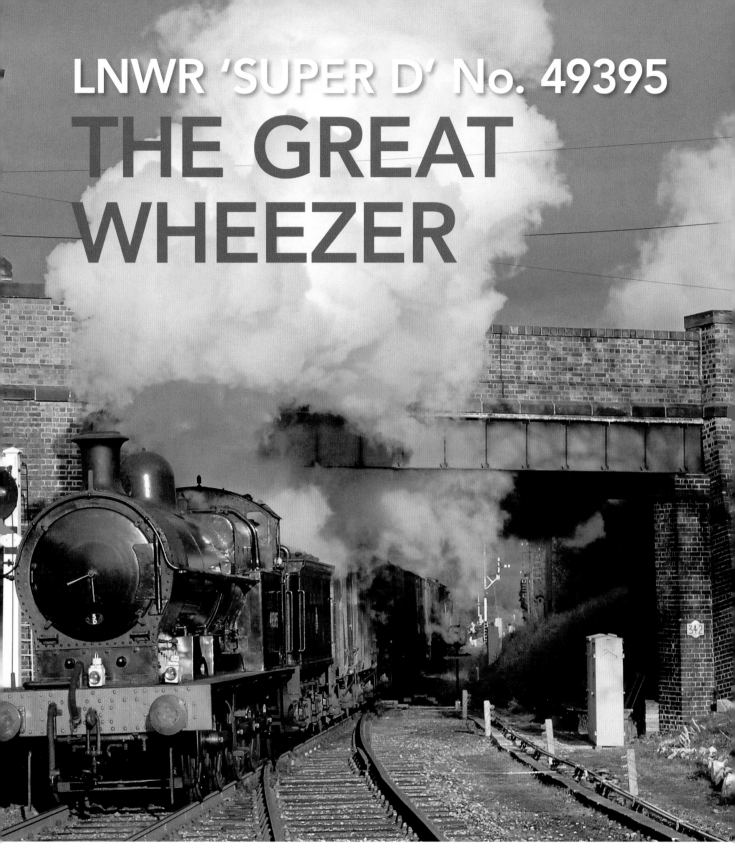

LNWR 'SUPER D' No. 49395
THE GREAT WHEEZER

with Belpaire boilers by the LMS from 1936 and became G2As, but some of the G2As received low-pressure boilers on overhaul, and reverted to Class G1. BR inherited 320 G2As, the largest ex-LNWR class to run on BR, but the G1s and G2As used the same number series.

Although these are the official LNWR, LMS and BR classifications for the engines, in LNWR days, all the 0-8-0 classes tended to be called Class D, whether they were or not, and those that received superheating were all known as 'Super Ds', a name that has stuck, among other less-flattering nicknames. Indeed,

the last development of the LNWR 0-8-0, the Belpaire-boilered two-cylindered G2A is far removed from actually being a 'Super D', which was a four-cylinder rebuild of an original Webb compound 0-8-0.

Needless to say, the evolution of what became known as the G2 class left many lineside observers confused.

PETER WATERMAN RESTEAMS THE LAST
The first of the new G2 class, No. 485, was selected for official preservation as the ultimate development of the 0-8-0

type by the LNWR, despite the LMS having developed the design further.

Withdrawn from Buxton shed as No. 49395 in very poor condition, after sustaining a cracked cylinder in an accident on the Ashbourne to Buxton line in 1959, it was stored at Crewe Works until it moved to Stratford in late 1964 or January 1965.

Sadly, the 'Super D' became one of the most neglected engines in the National Collection despite quickly being selected for display in a proposed new museum in Leicester. It moved to storage in the Midland roundhouse at Leicester in

LNWR 'Super D' No. 49395 passes Water Ark on the North Yorkshire Moors Railway in 2011. BRIAN SHARPE

November 1967.

However, when the museum's plans had to be scaled down, the G2 returned to the National Collection store, by now at Preston Park, in September 1970.

With the museum's plans resuscitated, No. 49395 moved back to Leicester in August 1972 but only for another four years' storage.

Its next move was to an engineering works locomotive shed at Horsehay near Telford on February 19, 1976, and might have seen the engine restored to work

on a heritage line being planned in the area, which became the Telford Steam Railway. However, instead, on September 14, 1981, it took a short journey to the Telford Industrial Museum at Blists Hill where at least it was on public view, although still no restoration took place.

The increasingly derelict hulk then moved to Tyseley Locomotive Works in 1988 and on to the Midland Railway Centre at Butterley, now the Midland Railway-Butterley, on July 4, 1990.

Sadly, the 'Super D' was widely

considered virtually beyond redemption by now.

However, a saviour appeared in 1993 in the form of Pete Waterman, who remembered the class with affection from his trainspotting days at Brinklow near Coventry. He offered to pay for the overhaul as new welding techniques were able to make an effective repair to the damaged cylinder.

No. 49395 was moved to the National Railway Museum that March and work finally started.

The cylinder was successfully repaired, but the restoration stalled and the deal between the museum and the Waterman Railway Heritage Trust was renegotiated in 1997 with Pete's modern-day London & North Western Railway outfit at Crewe taking over some of the work. The chassis was delivered in May 2002 for reassembly.

The 'Super D' ran from 2005-15, appearing on numerous heritage lines including the Great Central, Llangollen, Severn Valley, North Yorkshire Moors and Keighley & Worth Valley Railway, after undergoing running-in on the Churnet Valley Railway.

Pete reckoned he had spent the best part of £700,000 on returning it to steam – several times more than the original £125,000 estimate.

In March 2015, the locomotive was moved from storage at Buckley Wells on the East Lancashire Railway to the Locomotion museum at Shildon, where it was placed on display.

Built in 1921, LNWR G2 0-8-0 No. 49395 is seen on static display at the Locomotion museum in Shildon on January 8, 2016. ROB HODGKINS

Chapter 15

CAERPHILLY CASTLE
The one they can't paint!

Still in its coat of Brunswick green livery as applied by Swindon Works after its withdrawal, No. 4073 *Caerphilly Castle* is a star exhibit inside STEAM – Museum of the Great Western Railway at Swindon. ROBIN JONES

Eight GWR Castles survive in preservation, but one of them, No. 4073, has remained on static display for six decades as an example of one newly overhauled at a British Railways' workshop, which still has its coat of paint from then.

C harles Benjamin Collett's Castle 4-6-0 is one of the most powerful and famous locomotive types ever produced by the Great Western Railway.

Collett used Churchward's Star class four-cylindered 4-6-0 of 1906 as the basis for the new design. It had the basic layout of the Star with an extended frame and a newly designed No. 8 boiler, which was larger, but equally importantly lighter to keep within the stipulated axle load limit. It retained the long-travel valves and Belpaire firebox that had become the trademark of GWR express locomotives. There was an increase in tractive effort to 31,625lbs, and it was a locomotive that looked attractive and well-proportioned.

The first of the initial ordered batch of 10 was No. 4073 *Caerphilly Castle*, which emerged from Swindon in the summer of 1923, and made its debut at Paddington on August 23 that year. It was the first of a series that remained in production right up to 1950. Eventually 155 Castles were built new at Swindon; 15 were converted from Stars and Churchward's one-off Pacific No. 111 *The Great Bear* became a *Castle, Viscount Churchill.*

After a brief period of running-in service, between April and October 1924, *Caerphilly Castle* was exhibited at the British Empire Exhibition at Wembley Park alongside Nigel Gresley's new LNER A1 Pacific No. 4472 *Flying Scotsman*, with the GWR claiming that the Castle was Britain's most powerful express locomotive.

To add substance to his bold claim, GWR general manager, Sir Felix Pole, proposed to the LNER that an exchange trial of the two types should take place.

Accordingly, in April 1925, No. 4079 *Pendennis Castle* ran on the Great Northern main line and LNER A1 No. 4474 *Victor Wild* represented the LNER on the GW.

Most historians believe that the GWR locomotive won the battle in terms of speed, power and economy and this led to improvements being made to the LNER Pacific design. The GWR rather rubbed salt in the wound by sending *Pendennis Castle* straight to the British Empire Exhibition, which had reopened for the summer of 1925, where Pendennis stood alongside Scotsman, carrying a headboard proclaiming the Castle to be Britain's most powerful locomotive.

The LMS was also impressed with the Castle, having borrowed No. 5000 *Launceston Castle* for tests on the West Coast Main Line. It tried to either buy or borrow the drawings from Swindon to build its own but Swindon refused. The Castles achieved an enviable reputation for speed during the inter-war years on such trains as the then world's fastest, 'The Cheltenham Flyer'.

In 1946, Frederick Hawksworth, Collett's successor, introduced a higher degree of superheat, which resulted in increased economy, and from 1956 double chimneys were fitted by BR to some engines, combined with larger superheaters, and this significantly improved their performance.

The last three Castles were withdrawn from Gloucester in 1965. The last of all was No. 7029 *Clun Castle* in December 1965, which had worked BR's last steam train out of Paddington on November 27, 1965 and had outlasted the others by six months. It is preserved at Tyseley Locomotive Works.

IMMACULATE, BUT NEVER TO STEAM AGAIN

Caerphilly Castle's first shed allocation was Old Oak Common. In August 1950 it was at Bath Road, Bristol, and its last allocation was Cardiff Canton in March 1959 – a few months after it had been mechanically overhauled at its namesake Caerphilly Works. Withdrawn in May 1960, it was selected to be part of the National Collection, and was externally restored at Swindon Works at a cost of £11,000. Not only was it chosen because it was the first of its class, but it was in prime condition having been recently overhauled and also given a pristine paint job at the works where it had been built.

On June 2, 1961, No. 4073 was formally handed over by to the director of the Science Museum, Sir David Follett, by newly appointed British Railways chairman, Dr Richard Beeching, at Paddington station.

Pickfords hauled the engine to the museum in Kensington on Sunday June 4, where it was placed on display in the new extension, in the Land Transport section.

After the Science Museum decided to refurbish its displays, with its focus on switching moving and interactive exhibits, it was decided to transfer No. 4073 for display at the new STEAM – Museum of the Great Western Railway, which was being set up in part of the closed Swindon Works. While the work of setting up the museum was ongoing, No. 4073 was at first moved to Didcot on September 25, 1996.

After a further period on display at the National Railway Museum in York, it moved to Swindon on December 14, 1999 for the STEAM museum's opening.

The locomotive has never steamed in preservation despite it being in what is widely understood to be immaculate mechanical condition.

Any restoration to working order would inevitably damage its paintwork, which is now part of the locomotive's historical value, as it was applied by a BR works and has never undergone the wear and tear of what would be expected even in a week's normal service.

Nobody has ever made an issue of returning No. 4073 to steam. There are seven sister locomotives in preservation, six of which have run on the main line, so were would be the gain?

No. 6000 *King George V*
A KING TWICE OVER

No. 6000 *King George V* was the first of the Great Western Railway's legendary flagship class. It was also the locomotive that in 1971 ended British Rail's three-year ban on steam, paving the way for the vibrant charter market we enjoy today.

GWR Chief Mechanical Engineer, Charles Collett, who was far more an innovator than an inventor, continued with his predecessor George Churchward's basic design principles of narrow fireboxes, boilers with good circulation and high pressures with moderate levels of superheat.

While Collett's Castle 4-6-0s were a stunning success, by 1926 the demand for an even larger locomotive to serve the Swindon empire was apparent.

Collett was duly instructed by GWR's general manager, Sir Felix Pole, to go ahead with the design and construction of a 'Super-Castle', capable of hauling heavier expresses between Paddington and the West of England and the Midlands at average speeds around 60mph.

The King class, the first of which. No. 6000 *King George V*, emerged from Swindon Works in June 1927, was bigger than anything previously seen, and represented the ultimate development of Churchward's four-cylinder 4-6-0 concept. Churchward's preference for locomotive's without trailing wheels was in order to maximise adhesion on the notorious South Devon banks on the West of England main line to Plymouth, then the GWR's most important route, and who was Collett to challenge this basic design principle? The Kings were the heaviest 4-6-0s in Britain and had the

The bell presented to No. 6000 *King George V* by the Baltimore & Ohio Railroad has been carried ever since. ROBIN JONES

highest tractive effort.

Two months after it was outshopped, No. 6000 was shipped to the United States to feature in the Baltimore & Ohio Railroad's centenary celebrations that year. During the celebrations it was presented with a bell and a plaque, and these are carried to this day.

A total of 30 were built at Swindon in two batches in 1927-28 and 1930. Heavily restricted in view of their weight they

were mainly seen between Paddington and Plymouth and Paddington and Shrewsbury, their additional power being less needed on the more level routes to Bristol and South Wales.

The class was fitted with double chimneys and four-row superheaters in the 1950s, giving a marked improvement in performance and were recorded as comfortably exceeding 100mph on occasions.

No. 6000 *King George V* attained the highest-ever drawbar horsepower attained by a class member – 1951 edhp. Sister No. 6001 *King Edward VII* reached 109mph, the highest speed ever recorded by a King. Both were fitted with the four-row superheaters and double chimneys for their record runs.

However, despite their prowess, the magnificent Kings were an early target for withdrawal as the Western Region diesel-hydraulic classes came on stream in the early 1960s, and all of the Kings had gone by the end of 1962.

Remarkably though, No. 6018 *King Henry VI* was reinstated to work the Stephenson Locomotive Society 'Farewell to the Kings' railtour from Birmingham Snow Hill to Swindon on April 28, 1963.

Charles Collett continued the evolution of George Jackson Churchward's 4-6-0 designs to produce the Castles and Kings.

LEFT: GWR 4-6-0 No. 6000 *King George V* on display in the Great Hall of the National Railway Museum in 2010. ROBIN JONES

No. 6000 *King George V* at Old Oak Common in 1962. POLYRUS

No. 6000 departs from Hereford on the Newport-Chester 'Mayflower' special in April 1975.
HUGH LLEWELYN*

In scenes reminiscent of today's crowds flocking to see *Flying Scotsman*, *King George V*'s return-to-steam trips in October 1971 saw enthusiasts lining vantage points everywhere along the route. Here, No. 6000 heads towards Dorridge – then still known as Knowle & Dorridge – with the Hereford-Severn Tunnel Junction-Swindon-Oxford-Solihull-Tyseley leg on Saturday, October 2. ROBIN JONES

The return of the King – and of steam! No. 6000 *King George V* heads through Magor on October 2, 1971, the first leg of its comeback tour, following its overhaul sponsored by Hereford cider manufacturer's Bulmers. Behind it are the five Pullman coaches painted in Bulmers' umber-and-green livery that formed its exhibition train, to which three BR Mk.1 coaches were added.

No. 6000 *King George V* in BR Brunswick green livery with 1949 emblem at Bulmers' Steam Centre in Hereford in April 1974. HUGH LLEWELYN*

Two greats double-heading: LNER A3 Pacific No. 4472 *Flying Scotsman* leads GWR 4-6-0 No. 6000 *King George V* and the Bulmers' Pullman train at Grafton near Hereford with the Newport-Shrewsbury 'Atlantic Venturers Express' in September 1973. HUGH LLEWELYN*

No 6000 at Hereford on October 23, 1983.
POLYRUS*

Less than a year after the ban was lifted. *King George V* heads the Newport to Shrewsbury 'David & Charles Steam Special' at Llanvihangel Crucorney while climbing towards the summit of the Welsh Marches line in September 1972. HUGH LLEWELYN*

King George V passes Culham with the Up 'William Shakespeare Express' on a summer evening in the early 1980s. BARRY LEWIS*

SAVED FOR THE NATION

King George V was withdrawn in 1962 with 1,910,424 miles on the clock, and, as the first of the class, was officially preserved.

It was stored at Swindon until it moved to Stratford in December 1964, returning to Swindon on December 31, 1966.

After that, it was loaned to Hereford-based Bulmers Cider Ltd, which developed a now-closed railway heritage centre on its site.

In Bulmers' custody, No. 6000 was moved to an engineering works in Newport on August 9, 1968 for restoration to main line running order, despite BR's ban on the use of steam locomotives, which was imposed after the running of 1T57 the 'Fifteen Guinea Special' two days later.

The total ban on steam haulage excluded BR's 2ft gauge Vale of Rheidol Railway. The sole main line exception was No. 4472 *Flying Scotsman*.

King George V arrived at Hereford fully restored on November 13, 1968.

LIFTING THE BAN

The ban was slightly lifted to allow three preserved locomotives, including GWR Castle No. 7029 *Clun Castle*, to steam on a length of track at Cricklewood Depot open day in July 1969. However, total prohibition became effective when, later that year, *Flying Scotsman* embarked on an ill-fated tour of North America.

It seemed to everyone that live steam would from then on be confined

King George V exhibited in the Great Hall of the National Railway Museum on November 5, 2014.
ROBIN JONES

to heritage railways, which under the 1896 Light Railways Act are allowed to run trains at a maximum speed of only 25mph.

As the preservation movement gathered strength, pressure was brought to bear on BR to allow limited workings by privately owned locomotives. The Association of Railway Preservation Societies, forerunner of today's Heritage Railway Association, began holding talks with British Rail about relaxing the ban.

A breakthrough came when Richard Marsh became chairman of the British Railways Board in 1971.

Peter Prior, then managing director of Bulmers, wanted to see No. 6000 the five-coach Bulmer's Pullman exhibition train (painted in Bulmers' green and brown livery) on a promotional tour of the country.

He got his way. BR finally relented, and agreed to a trial running by No 6000.

On September 13, 1971, *King George V* was approved for main line running by inspector Norman Tovey, and two days later, underwent an unannounced trial run to Newport.

No. 6000 made a four-day tour of the Western Region, taking in Kensington Olympia and Birmingham in early October 1971. Three British Rail Mk.1 coaches were added to the Bulmers' Pullman rake for fare-paying passengers. Amazingly, the fare was only £5.

The route of the special with driver, Ron Wargen, and fireman Derek Foster on the footplate, with Jack Temple as chief inspector, included London, Swindon, Newport and Birmingham,

and hundreds of thousands of people, including the author, flocked to the lineside to see it.

It was a triumph for steam, and for Swindon engineering.

Two days later, it headed a second 'Return to Steam' special, this time from Birmingham Moor Street to Kensington Olympia. A third special was run on October 7 from London to Hereford.

THE DOOR REOPENS

As a result of the success of these trips, British Rail agreed to open 300 miles of main line to steam and approved 23 preserved locomotives for use on them.

BR announced its very limited 'Return to Steam' commencing in June 1972.

The rules were; lightly used routes, suitable steam locomotive based nearby, triangle or other turning facility at each end. BR had removed all steam infrastructure, few turntables existed and virtually no watering facilities.

The return to the main line of *King George V* is widely credited as the beginning of today's main line steam scene, and as such, is a major landmark, not only in preservation, but in terms of UK transport history and the nation's tourist economy.

The decanting of 500 passengers for the day in places like Scarborough, Swanage and Minehead does not go unnoticed by traders, especially when such tours take place outside the main holiday season, and look at the enormous contribution made to the West Highland tourist economy by West Coast Railways' summer walk-on Fort William to Mallaig

'Jacobite' services.

King George V was to haul many more charters and also participated in the Paddington 125 celebrations in 1979 and GW150 in 1985

However, Kings were heavily restricted even on GWR lines because of their size, and although No. 6000 found itself on one or two Western Region routes, which never saw class members in steam days, it was never permitted outside the WR system.

MUSEUM LIFE

After 16 years of running, the National Railway Museum decided not to proceed with a costly overhaul of No. 6000 because another member of the class, the privately preserved No. 6024 *King Edward I*, had become operational.

Furthermore, while No. 6024 has had its height reduced to conform to today's main line specifications, No. 6000 remains in its original condition.

No. 6000 had a final run from Swindon to Hereford on September 26, 1987 and retired to static display, while No. 6024 was returned to service in 1990.

No. 6000 has been on display either at the National Railway Museum at York or at the STEAM museum in Swindon.

The third survivor of the class, the Great Western society's No. 6023 *King Edward II*, which was, like No. 6024, restored from Barry scrapyard condition, has also been restored to running order.

It has been painted in BR's short-lived express passenger blue livery, and in 2017 was being prepared for main line running.

MALLARD
TOP OF THE WORLD

In 1802, Richard Trevithick experimented with a self-propelled engine on rails at Coalbrookdale in Shropshire, one of the cradles of the Industrial Revolution, and gave the steam locomotive concept to the world. Fast forward 136 years, and Britain reached the pinnacle of the steam age, when Sir Nigel Gresley's streamlined A4 Pacific reached 126mph, and set an all-time global record, which has yet to be broken, and probably never will. *Mallard* today is not only a prime exhibit in the National Railway Museum at York, but a garter blue-liveried source of British pride.

LNER streamlined A4 Pacific No. 4468 *Mallard* stands at York station with a special in April 1988. The locomotive was, as the headboard suggests, returned to steam to celebrate the 40th anniversary of its world record run that year.
BRIAN SHARPE

On July 3, 1938 a private steam train waited on the East Coast Main Line at Barkston South Junction three miles north of Grantham, in readiness for its return journey to London.

Before the whistle was sounded for its departure, at 2.49pm, everyone on board was told, for the first time on the journey, what was the true nature of the trip, and offered a taxi to Peterborough if they did not wish to ride on it.

Not one of them took up the option, choosing to remain on board whatever the consequences.

For this was not an ordinary breaking test train, as they had been led to believe, before it had set out from Wood Green sidings in north London.

It was nothing less than an all-out attempt by the LNER to snatch the world steam speed record from Nazi Germany.

The garter-blue locomotive was streamlined A4 No. 4468 *Mallard*.

And within an hour, it would have achieved a feat that would make it a household name across the world.

THE ROAD TO IMMORTALITY

The real journey had not begun at Wood Green that day, but five years previously.

It was in 1933, a year before *Flying Scotsman* officially reached 100mph, that Nigel Gresley, visited Germany and experienced the new high-speed streamlined 'Flying Hamburger' two-car diesel units for himself. Operating between Berlin and Hamburg at 99mph, they quickly became the fastest train in the world, signalling an end to steam as the predominant form of traction on the world's railways.

Impressive, yes, but in the Thirties, steam was still more cost effective, and engineers looked in depth at ways in which the aerodynamic advantages of streamlining could also be applied to conventional locomotives.

German locomotive builder, Henschel-Werke, subsequently produced an express steam train that could compete with the 'Flying Hamburger'. Gresley

The 'Silver Jubilee' was the LNER's first streamlined train as it invested heavily in fast express services in the Thirties. ROBIN JONES COLLECTION

rode on one, and was wowed.

LNER chief general manager, Sir Ralph Wedgwood, wondered whether with an ordinary Pacific steam locomotive, even faster overall speeds could be maintained with a train of much greater weight, capacity, and comfort.

Streamlining was seen as the key to it all; the next big step forward in steam locomotive evolution. Its perceived purpose was not only to reduce air

The plaque fixed to *Mallard* commemorating its world steam speed record on July 3, 1938. ROBIN JONES

resistance at high speed, but to boost the glamour appeal of big fast steam locomotives for publicity purposes. Long gone were the days that the public were worried about fast trains, and *City of Truro's* feat on Wellington Bank in 1904 had had to be hushed up.

Following trials in 1935 with A3 Pacifics No. 2750 *Papyrus*, which recorded a new maximum of 108mph, Wedgwood authorised Gresley to produce a streamlined development of the A3.

Four locomotives comprise the first batch, all with the word 'silver' as part of their names. The first was No. 2509 *Silver Link*, followed by No. 2510 *Quicksilver*, No. 2511 *Silver King* and No. 2512 *Silver Fox*. Their utterly non-conventional shape – for which Gresley had received initial inspiration from a Bugatti racing car – startled an unsuspecting public and in a split second destroyed anyone's notion of what a steam locomotive should look like.

The locomotives' air-smoothed casings were matched by seven coaches painted silver with valances between the wheels. And so a new streamlined train, the 'Silver Jubilee' was built.

Waiting for the signal: No. 4468 *Mallard* is all set to try for the world speed record as it stands ready at Barkston South Junction on July 3, 1938. RAIL ARCHIVE STEPHENSON

Deutsche Reichsbahn Class 05 4-6-4 No. 05001, the surviving sister of No. 05002, which set a world steam speed record in 1936. It is preserved in the DB Museum in Nuremberg. ROBIN JONES

The design of the new Pacific locomotive to haul it, designated an A4 – the next in the evolutionary line after the A1/A3 4-6-2s – had art deco wedge-shaped streamlining that had been refined with the assistance of Professor Dalby and the wind tunnel facilities at the National Physical Laboratory at Teddington.

The A4s were designed for high-speed passenger services. The application of internal streamlining to the steam circuit, higher boiler pressure and the extension of the firebox to form a combustion chamber all contributed to a more efficient locomotive than the A3. Consumption of both coal and water were reduced.

A trial run on September 27, 1935 saw *Silver Link*, then just three weeks old, twice reach 112mph and sustain an average speed of 100mph for 43 consecutive miles on the East Coast Main Line.

The 'Silver Jubilee' made the A4s an overnight success, and led to other streamlined services being introduced: the 'Coronation' (London-Edinburgh, July 1937) and the 'West Riding Limited' (Bradford & Leeds-London and return, November 1937) for which more A4s were built.

SERVING AN EVIL EMPIRE

Across the North Sea, Germany's Borsig locomotive works built three streamlined steam locomotives, which became that country's Class 05.

The second of these, No. 05002, seized the world steam locomotive speed record on May 11, 1936, when it reached 124.5mph while hauling a 197-ton train on the Berlin-Hamburg line.

This speed record was not set intentionally, but came about as a result of an order from the Deutsche Reichsbahn hierarchy to the locomotive crew in order to impress a party of Nazi top brass on board.

The German state railway saw Hitler's promotion of autobahns as the transport of the future, and desperately wanted to highlight the fact that trains could still have a big part to play in his Third Reich.

The passengers on that trip included Heinrich Himmler and Reinhard Heydrich, who were indeed inspired by railways. These architects of the Holocaust used railways as the means of transporting of millions of innocent people to their deaths in concentration camps.

Hitler's earlier Aktion T4 programme of euthanasia, primarily directed at eradicating disabled and mentally ill people in Germany, was ended in August 1941, with the Fuhrer taking the very rare step of bowing to outraged public opinion in his own country.

At the same time, he realised that if the Nazis wanted to exterminate people they would need to do it out of sight of the German public. Occupied Eastern Europe was the ideal setting. There was, of course, no internet or similar form of mass communication in those days to let the general public know what was really going on, and the press could be controlled, and so mass deportation trains became the essential means to their end.

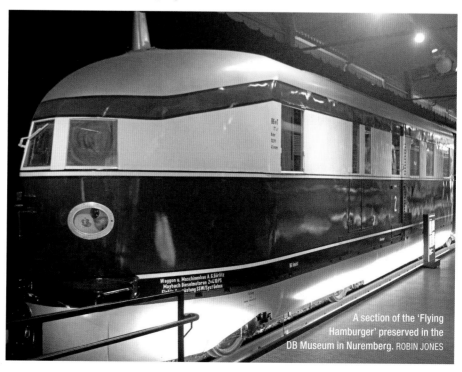

A section of the 'Flying Hamburger' preserved in the DB Museum in Nuremberg. ROBIN JONES

Mallard reaching 126mph on Stoke Bank, as captured on film by an LNER lineside technician on July 3, 1938. NRM

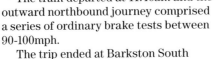

The recording equipment inside the LNER dynamometer car. ROBIN JONES

THE GOLDEN MOMENT

A further improvement to the A4 design was the fitting of a Kylchap double-blastpipe chimney, which was first introduced on No. 4468 *Mallard*, built in March 1938, and was eventually applied to all class members.

The LNER wanted badly to regain that speed crown, but Gresley knew that by increasing locomotive speeds, braking distances were becoming longer.

He realised that he needed to source a more effective braking system, and so he arranged trials of the Westinghouse system used by his rival the LMS.

So on July 3, 1938, the Westinghouse team arrived at London's Wood Green depot to find *Mallard* steamed up and coupled to the LNER's teak dynamometer car to record the speed, with LNER test inspector Denis Carling in charge of the recording equipment set. Behind that were three twin sets of carriages from the LNER's luxury new 'Coronation'.

Illness meant that Gresley missed the trip, and he delegated his deputy Douglas Edge to oversee proceedings.

At the outset, the true purpose of the run was kept secret from the footplate crew, headed by 61-year-old veteran Doncaster driver, Joe Duddington, who had a reputation for running trains hard when needed. Also on the footplate were fireman Tommy Bray and traction inspector Sam Jenkins.

The train departed at 11.46am and the outward northbound journey comprised a series of ordinary brake tests between 90-100mph.

The trip ended at Barkston South Junction, where the true purpose of the tip was revealed after lunch in the restaurant car.

Planners had worked out that that a good run from Barkston would allow *Mallard* to climb Stoke Bank at speed, with the world record being attempted on the downwards gradient.

The train set off at 4.15pm.

However, Duddington and his crew were dismayed to find a 'dead slow' track-maintenance speed limit in force at Grantham. Accordingly, *Mallard* passed through the station at a dismal 18mph.

Undeterred, Bray made the best use of delay to stoke up a big fire, and beyond Grantham, *Mallard* reached 65mph, and accelerated up to Stoke summit where it passed the signalbox at 85mph; 6mph better than *Silver Fox* when it set its record.

Inside Stoke Tunnel, there was a firework display of red-hot cinders flying from *Mallard's* twin chimneys past the carriage windows.

With the summit conquered *Mallard* then accelerated down the gradient of Stoke Bank, way in excess of the official 90mph limit.

The speedometer reached 120mph,

bettering the best that the LMS had done so far.

It was at milepost 90¼, between Little Bytham and Essendine, that the equipment in the dynamometer car recorded 126mph.

Mallard thundered through Little Bytham station, spraying hot ashes as well as breaking windows, and crockery on board the train. No matter. Nazi Germany's speed record was no more.

Edge was asked if 130mph should be attempted, but he erred on the side of caution through the intercom set up between the dynamometer car and the footplate, and ordered Duddington to slow down.

After Essendine station was passed at 108mph, a distinctive odour was noticed by the engine crew, *Mallard's* big end had run hot. When the train stopped at Peterborough, it was found that the white metal had melted, nearly wrecking the locomotive. It was left to an ageing Ivatt Atlantic, No. 3290, to head the train back to King's Cross after *Mallard* had been taken off.

Edge rang the absent Gresley to tell him of the success, and within hours, *Mallard's* feat was generating global front page news. The press coined the nickname 'Blue Streak' for *Mallard*: afterwards all A4s became known as 'streaks'. From then on, every schoolboy longed to become an engine driver.

In Germany, there was deafening silence about *Mallard's* triumph.

For me, the greatest aspect of the record run was the unintended symbolism. On the front of the prestige locomotives of the Reichsbahn at that time was fixed the Nazi swastika with an all-powerful golden eagle mounted above the badge.

Yet on that Sunday, that proud and mighty take-no-prisoners eagle was beaten into second place, for all time, by a commonplace river and pond duck, a species that never sought to hurt anyone. For me, that is so wonderfully typical of Britain, and indeed humanity at its best.

Gresley was convinced that an A4 could do 130mph, but his plans for another test run were stopped by the outbreak of the Second World War.

The carriage that recorded both *Flying Scotsman's* 100mph run and *Mallard's* world record: the LNER's teak dynamometer car inside the Great Hall of the National Railway Museum at York. ROBIN JONES

As No. 60022, *Mallard* heads the 'Tyne-Tees Pullman' in the British Railways era. ROBIN JONES

EVERYDAY SERVICE
FOR THE LIVING LEGEND

A total of 34 A4s were built. *Mallard* continued in service for another quarter of a century after its world-beating white metal-melting run.

Its streamlined valances were removed in spring 1942 to ease maintenance and it was repainted into wartime black. The valances were restored in preservation.

The distinctive A4 chime whistles were removed from the A4s in 1942 and destroyed because the government believed that they could become confused with air-raid sirens.

No. 4468 was based at Doncaster until October 21, 1943, when it was reallocated to Grantham. Under the renumbering system of Gresley's successor Edward Thompson, it became No. 22. After Nationalisation in 1948, it was repainted into garter blue as British Railways No. E22 and on September 16. 1949, it became No. 60022.

In 1948, the Locomotive Exchanges were held, with engines from one Big Four company trialled on the former territory of another, in order to establish which were best in terms of speed, power and efficiency with coal and water. Collected data was used to draw up new designs for the planned Standard series of locomotives, of which 999 were eventually built.

On June 8, 1948, *Mallard* ran on the Waterloo-Exeter route. Despite being held back by a succession of red signals, its train was only 5½ minutes late, and at Axminster, it had reached 82mph.

Mallard's final reallocation was to King's Cross or 'Top Shed' on April 11, 1948. It was given a new corridor tender and headed non-stop expresses to Scotland. In mid-1952, the garter blue livery was replaced with BR lined Brunswick green.

On September 8, 1961 *Mallard* headed the final non-stop 'The Elizabethan' from King's Cross to Edinburgh Waverley. It completed the 392 ¾-mile journey nearly three minutes early, despite five permanent way slacks and two signal checks.

No. 60022's finest postwar moment came on September 19, 1961, when it produced one of the highest power outputs reached by an A4 when it hauled the 2pm from King's Cross to Newcastle with 11 coaches.

Up the 1-in-440 gradient from Tallington to Essendine on Stoke Bank, scene of its greatest triumph, it reached 78mph, and 82mph as the slopes eased beyond to Corby Glen. The estimated drawbar horse power (edhp) would have been around 2150, very high indeed for an A4, even those fitted with a Kylchap chimney. It reached the 1-in-178 summit at 78mph, where 50-60mph was par for the course.

Thereby, it achieved a unique double-record run up the legendary incline, as opposed to down it.

Mallard returned to the Waterloo-Exeter line for a Locomotive Club of Great Britain railtour on February 24, 1963, and was withdrawn from King's Cross on April 25 that year, after it had covered 1,426,261 miles.

Mallard had been equipped with 12 different boilers and seven tenders during its 25-year career.

SPEED OVER SENIORITY

When a particular locomotive type was identified for preservation as part of the National Collection, the usual practice was that the first in the class would be chosen.

Clearly the collection was to include an A4, and under that practice, No. 60014 (2509) *Silver Link*, the first in the class, and the second most famous, should have been saved.

However, it was the later *Mallard* that held the world record, and an exception to the rule saved it.

Mallard went into Doncaster Works for external restoration to original condition, complete with valances and garter blue livery as No. 4468, and was earmarked for the new Museum of British Transport at Clapham, which it entered on February 29, 1964.

Withdrawn on December 29, 1962, the Eastern Region was unwilling to sell *Silver Link*, and quoted holiday camp magnate Billy Butlin too high a price. Somewhat disgracefully, *Silver Link* was scrapped and lost to a nation that would have treasured it.

Clapham Museum proved short lived, and was superseded by the National Railway Museum at York. *Mallard* was back on the main line when it was towed from London to York for static display on April 12, 1975.

In 1977, *Mallard* was displayed at York to mark the station's centenary. During June 17-18, 1978, it visited Doncaster Works for an open day commemorating the 12th anniversary of The Plant.

In April 2012, *Mallard* was taken to Barrow Hill for the Chesterfield venue's 'Fab Four' LNER-themed gala, and is seen sandwiched between (left to right) operational sister *Bittern*, A1 Pacific No. 60163 *Tornado*, A2 Pacific No. 60532 *Blue Peter* and V2 2-6-2 No. 4771 *Green Arrow*. ROBIN JONES

Mallard thunders through Clapham in North Yorkshire with a special in May 1986. ROBIN JONES

STEAMING AGAIN

With the 1988 half-centenary of its record run approaching, the NRM decided to return *Mallard* to steam.

The Friends of the National Railway Museum established a Mallard 88 working party and gained support from Scarborough Borough Council, which was backing the launch of BR's 'Scarborough Spa Express' specials that year.

The resort stumped up around $35,000 towards the cost of the restoration of *Mallard* in the former diesel depot next to the Leeman Road museum which, it had just acquired. A specialist contractor extracted the asbestos lagging from around the boiler.

A pair of gearboxes for the Flanan speed recorder was obtained from the French Railway Museum at Mulhouse to replace the wooden mock-ups installed for museum display purposes.

In order to obtain an unconditional boiler certificate for main line running, many firebox stays would have had to have been replaced at great cost. However, one way around this was to restrict the locomotive to a limited number of operating days.

Marking the tenth anniversary of the NRM, Mallard moved under its own power, minus its boiler cladding, on September 27, 1985 and it returned to the main line on March 25 1986, hauling

a special train from York to Doncaster via Scarborough and Hull as a test run. It ran its first heritage-era main line railtour on July 9, 1986, when it hauled British Rail's 'Scarborough Spa Express' from York to Scarborough and back via Hull and Goole. It reached 74.5mph at Copmanthorpe.

On October 4, 1986, *Mallard* ran from York to Marylebone via Sheffield, Derby, Birmingham and Banbury. It then hauled three dining train trips, from Marylebone to Stratford-upon-Avon and back on October 12, 26 and November 4.

May 16, 1987 saw *Mallard* hauling – appropriately in view of its designer's hobby, which saw many of the A4s named after wild birds – an RSPB special from Carnforth to York.

On October 2, *Mallard* joined forces with BR Standard 9F 2-10-0 No. 92220 *Evening Star*, the last main line steam locomotive built by British Railways, for a trip from York to Doncaster. The next day, both attended a Doncaster Works open day before returning to their York home.

The world record half-century celebrations for *Mallard* were staged in 1988. On May 9, it headed a Post Office special from Marylebone to Banbury, carrying a 'Postal Pullman' headboard. The train not only marked 150 years of sorting mail on the move but also the release of four stamps featuring

transport in the Thirties, one, the 18p, depicting *Mallard*.

Several members of the original train crew from July 3, 1938 were tracked down and invited to join a special excursion from Doncaster to Scarborough on the exact 50th anniversary.

BR chairman, Sir Peter Parker, agreed for *Mallard* to take over from an electric locomotive on the East Coast Main Line north of Doncaster, for a run to Scarborough.

On board the special were driver Joe Duddington's granddaughter Jean Delaney, and her son Matthew, and Tom Bray, the son of the fireman. Thousands packed the lineside to glimpse *Mallard* pass at 60mph on the trip.

Mallard steamed for the last time on August 27, 1988, and has since then remained a static exhibit. On July 26-27, 2003, *Mallard* was taken out of the museum and displayed at an open weekend at Doncaster Works to mark its 150th anniversary.

On the weekend of July 5-6, 2008, *Mallard* was brought outside the NRM and displayed alongside the three other preserved A4s in Britain, No. 4464/60019 *Bittern*, No. 60007 *Sir Nigel Gresley*, which set a postwar steam speed record of 112mph on Stoke Bank on May 23, 1959, and No. 60009 *Union of South Africa*, to mark the 70th anniversary of the world record.

STEAM'S GREATEST GATHERING OF ALL?

To many people, the word 'museum' invokes thought of a stuffy, dull and boring collection of exhibits. However, at the NRM and its outreach station of the Locomotion Museum in Shildon, nothing could be further from the truth.

For during a period of transatlantic curatorial excellence, all six surviving A4s were reunited to mark the 75th anniversary of the world record.

Yes, all six, including two which, by virtue of their names, found themselves on static display in north American museums following withdrawal by British Railways in the mid-Sixties.

No. 60008 *Dwight D. Eisenhower* was cosmetically restored at Doncaster on July 19, 1963, before it was shipped across the Atlantic to New York, and arrived at the National Railroad Museum in Green Bay, Wisconsin in May

the following year. There, it is displayed with two restored British carriages once used as part of Eisenhower's Command Train.

No. 60010 *Dominion of Canada* was donated by BR to the Canadian Railroad Historical Association and since May 1966 has been a resident of Exporail, the Canadian Railway Museum at Delson/Saint-Constant, Quebec, near Montreal.

As the British railway heritage movement grew in both stature and resources, several offers were made to buy these A4s from their overseas museum homes, but all such offers were rebuffed.

However, National Railway Museum director, Steve Davies, formulated a plan to borrow both of them in exchange for their cosmetic refurbishment, in order to celebrate the 75th anniversary of *Mallard's* world-record run. Once the Mallard 75 celebrations were over, they

would be shipped back. Everyone would gain, but there was an army of sceptics who said it would never happen.

But happen it did.

Andrew Goodman, whose Moveright International firm, based near Sutton Coldfield, specialises in the transport of railway locomotives and rolling stock by road, predominantly for heritage lines, joined the Mallard 75 sponsors, and flew out to North America to see what needed to be done. To cut a very long and extremely complicated story short, he oversaw their return to the UK.

After a journey from their museum homes lasting several weeks and beset by delays, both A4s were loaded aboard an Atlantic Container Line cargo ship at Halifax, Nova Scotia, on September 25, 2012, and docked at Liverpool Freeport a week later. Dawn on October 3 saw both being unloaded from the ship.

They were taken by low-loaded across the Pennines to the Locomotion museum in Shildon, where the restorations of both locomotives were to be started.

However, it was not only Nos. 60008 and 60010 in need of cosmetic restoration.

Lancashire-based Heritage Painting, which had built up a superb track record with repainting classic steam locomotives, was contracted to apply a new coat of garter-blue livery to *Mallard*, the paintwork of which had become somewhat jaded, before starting on *Dwight D. Eisenhower* after it had been brought from Locomotion to join its sister.

At part of the Mallard 75 celebrations, Jeremy Hosking's main line operational arm, Locomotive Services Limited, obtained special dispensation from Network Rail to run his A4, No. 4464 *Bittern*, at 90mph on three passenger-carrying trips over the East Coast Main Line, the current speed limit on the UK rail network being 75mph.

As near to Stoke Bank as a static locomotive can be displayed: *Mallard* on a specially laid siding at Grantham station on September 8, 2013. ROBIN JONES

On June 29, 2013, heading the first of the trips, 'The Ebor Streak', from King's Cross to York, *Bittern* reached its top speed of 92.5mph south of Newark Northgate. After arriving at York, *Bittern* and its support coach were uncoupled and moved into museum's north yard, ready to take its place around the turntable in the Great Hall for the Great Gathering of all six A4s.

At 8am on Wednesday, July 3 – 75 years to the day of the record run – *Mallard* sounded its trademark chime whistle before being shunted by the NRM's Class 08 diesel shunter into the Great Hall from the yard outside as the York Railway Institute Brass Band played a fanfare.

No. 4468 was shunted on to the turntable, before it was positioned alongside its sister locomotives *Sir Nigel Gresley, Dwight D. Eisenhower, Union of South Africa, Bittern* and *Dominion of Canada*.

On that opening day, around 7000 visitors entered the Great Hall to see the six in place.

Enthusiasts from all over the world, including Australia, Canada, the USA, and even Norfolk Island, a remote island in the South Pacific, amassed to celebrate *Mallard's* anniversary.

Paul Kirkman, who had by then replaced Steve Davies as museum head, opened the event with a speech. He said: "Seventy-five years ago to this day, this mighty machine raced down Stoke Bank near Grantham at the incredible speed of 126mph. That placed a permanent marker on the international timeline for British technological excellence, and it's a record still held today.

"Not only was it a marvellous feat of engineering but it was also a triumph of British design. *Mallard's* technical ability is surpassed only by its beauty.

"It has earned its place in the hearts of millions and to me sums up everything great about British innovation: both our vision to be the best and our ability to achieve it."

A record-breaking 13,035 people passed through the museum's doors on the first Saturday of the Great Gathering, which ran until July 17. The overall attendance was 138,141, making the event the most successful in the history of the museum.

Prince Charles visited on July 22, climbing on to *Mallard's* footplate and sounding the whistle powered by an air compressor. He had entered the Great Hall on a special train headed by *Bittern*, carrying the Prince of Wales' coat of arms.

For the weekend of September 7-8, *Mallard* was towed by a diesel down the ECML to the point nearest to Stoke Bank where it could be publicly displayed. A siding was relaid at Grantham station to house the A4 alongside one of its mighty

The most successful series of events in the National Railway Museum's history was Mallard 75. Here, all six surviving A4s are grouped around the turntable on July 3, 2013, the 75th anniversary of the world record. Left to right are *Sir Nigel Gresley, Dwight D. Eisenhower, Union of South Africa, Bittern, Dominion of Canada* and *Mallard*. ROBIN JONES

Prince Charles on the footplate of *Mallard* during his visit to the National Railway Museum on July 22, 2013, as part of Mallard 75. ROBIN JONES

Mallard briefly appeared in black livery during its cosmetic refurbishment at the National Railway Museum in the summer of 2012 in time for the Mallard 75 events the following year. ROBIN JONES

The Great Goodbye at the Locomotion museum in Shildon in February 2014: an evening view, which has become a seminal image of UK railway preservation. From left to right are *Sir Nigel Gresley*, *Dwight D. Eisenhower*, *Union of South Africa*, *Dominion of Canada*, *Bittern* and *Mallard*. FRED KERR

June 19, 2017 saw a bronze plaque dedicated to Sir Nigel Gresley unveiled on the house where he was born in 1876; 32 Dublin Street in Edinburgh. He was born in the Scottish capital only because his mother had gone there to see a gynaecologist. The family home was at Netherseal in Derbyshire where he grew up. GRESLEY SOCIETY

Mallard 75 earned the National Railway Museum the top honour in the sector, the Heritage Railway Association's Peter Manisty Award for Excellence 2014. Proudly holding the 2014 award in front of No. 4468 *Mallard* are Tony Oldfield, day-to-day manager of the Mallard 75 event, Mark Smith, chairman of the HRA awards committee, Tobias Lumb, the NRM's head of public programmes and project manager of Mallard 75, Dave MacLean, a former signal man who was heavily involved in providing cab access during the Great Gatherings at York, museum director Paul Kirkman, and Dave Hurd who managed the locomotive cleaning team. ROBIN JONES

modern traction successors, Class 55 Deltic No. 55019 *Royal Highland Fusilier*, as the centrepiece of the local Story of Speed festival.

A second event, the Autumn Great Gathering was held at the museum, for 17 days from October 26, and this time attracted 108,419 visitors.

Meanwhile, *Bittern's* second 90mph trips, rearranged for December 5 that year, saw it haul the 'Tyne Tees Streak' from York to Newcastle and back leg, purportedly reaching 94mph on the 1-in-220 downgrade to Parkgate Junction, and a passenger's GPS device recorded 95mph, although Locomotive Services Ltd said the true speed had been 93mph.

The third and final Mallard 75 event featuring all six A4s lined up – the Great Goodbye – was staged at Locomotion, between February 15-23 attracting 119,880 visitors.

The repatriated pair stayed on display until Easter, when Andrew Goodman oversaw their return to North America.

Thanks in part to sponsorship deals, Mallard 75 made more than £500,000 profit for the NRM's parent organisation the Science Museum by attracting 365,000 visitors.

So what does the future hold for *Mallard*?

There seems little justification at the moment for funding a return to running order. June 2017 saw *Union of South Africa* return to the main line after 18 months' absence, although owner, John Cameron, has indicated it may well be retired as a static museum exhibit once its 10-year boiler ticket runs out. No. 60007, owned by the Sir Nigel Gresley Locomotive Trust Limited, was, at the time of writing, undergoing an overhaul in the National Railway Museum's workshops at York. *Bittern* was also withdrawn in 2015 and being overhauled at Crewe.

So, it seems that for the foreseeable future, there will be at least one, if not two A4s, in operation hauling special trains over the national network. Would there be a market for a third? Probably not.

However, when the centenary of the world speed record run comes round on July 3, 2038, it is likely to be a very different story. There may be many who will say that nothing less than a resteaming of *Mallard* will suffice for the great occasion.

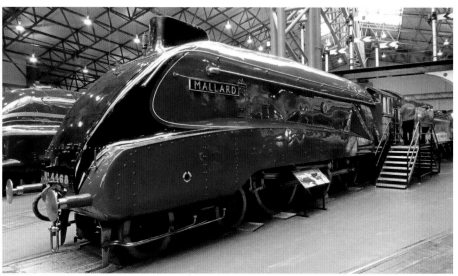

Mallard on display in the National Railway Museum today. ROBIN JONES

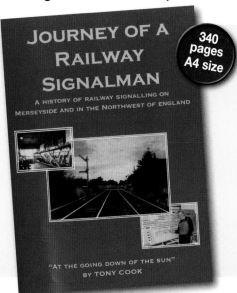

Duchess of HAMILTON

The big red bulbous one!

As we have seen, the Races to the North between the east and west coast routes between London and Scotland in Victorian times were rekindled in the Thirties.

The east coast had Gresley and his Pacifics, but hard on their heels was William Stanier of the London, Midland & Scottish Railway, who had been poached from the Great Western Railway to become Chief Mechanical Engineer on January 1, 1932, and was delegated with the task of ridding the Big Four company of its inherited Midland Railway small-engine policy and designing new, modern, and far more powerful locomotives.

One of his most successful LMS designs was the 'Black Five' mixed-traffic 4-6-0, which has been described as the best all-purpose steam locomotive ever to appear on Britain's railways.

Another stunner was Stanier's 8F 2-8-0, a freight version of the 'Black Five'. A total of 852 were built, with the locomotive works of other Big Four companies turning them out for the war Department and service overseas during the Second World War.

Between 1934-36, 191 of Stanier's Jubilee 4-6-0s, so named after the Silver Jubilee of King George V in 1935, were built.

All of these were magnificent classes in their own right, but for Stanier, the best by far was yet to come.

In response to Gresley's record-breaking innovations on the East Coast Main Line, including *Flying Scotsman's* headline-grabbing 100mph, and then the streamlined A4 Pacifics, Stanier's rival programme included the building of three prototype 4-6-2s.

The first, No. 6200 *The Princess Royal*, was completed on June 27, 1933, and led to two batches of locomotives being built. There was a first batch of two, including No. 6201 *Princess Elizabeth*, named after the future Queen, and a second batch of 11. The official name for the class, the Princess Royal, was selected because Mary, who held that title, was the Commander-in-Chief of the Royal Scots, but they became popularly known as 'Lizzies'.

Stanier's team drew up plans for a six-hour non-stop service between Euston and Glasgow Central to take on the LNER's similarly timed services, and in the process set a new Anglo-Scottish record. First, however, a trial run had to place to prove it was feasible.

Tom Clark, the senior driver from 5A Crewe North shed, from where locomen worked south to London and north to Perth, was chosen and No. 6201 *Princess Elizabeth* was rostered to run the test train from Euston to Glasgow Central.

On November 16, 1936, Tom Clark and his crew drove the train, designated 703, and weighing 225 tons, from Euston to Glasgow in five hours 53mins 38secs. It was the longest non-stop journey with a steam locomotive that had been performed at that time.

The restreamlined LMS Princess Coronation Pacific No. 6229 *Duchess of Hamilton* added a new dimension to Britain's heritage locomotive collection, for it recreated an outline that had not been seen for six decades when it was unveiled on May 20, 2009. ROBIN JONES

At a glance, one of the most striking locomotives inside the National Railway Museum, and indeed in the entire National Collection, is restreamlined Princess Coronation Pacific No. 6229 *Duchess of Hamilton*. Yet it was not always in that form by any means. ROBIN JONES

Princess Royal 4-6-2 No. 6201 *Princess Elizabeth*, in an official LMS photograph. This locomotive has survived into preservation where it has been a popular performer for decades, but it has never been part of the National Collection. ROBIN JONES COLLECTION

Next day, the trio completed the return journey in five hours 44mins 14secs. On arrival back at Euston, the footplate trio were taken to Broadcasting House and interviewed by the BBC. There, they were feted as national heroes, and suddenly, every schoolboy in Britain wanted to be the next Tom Clark.

THE 'BIG LIZZIES'

The LMS directors and their Chief Mechanical Engineer knew that they were right to produce the blueprint for a new Anglo-Scottish express, to be named the 'Coronation Scot'.

In a bid to grab the British speed record for the LMS, Stanier looked at building on the success of his Princess Royals by designing, what was in effect, an enlarged version to match or even better the A4s.

Influenced by the reception given to Gresley's striking A4s, he added streamlining to the design.

The result: the first of 38 new streamlined Princess Coronation class Pacifics, No. 6220 *Coronation*, which emerged from Crewe Works on June 1, 1937.

At 3300hp, they were the most powerful passenger steam locomotives ever built for the British railway network.

You could draw parallels between Gresley's A1/A3s and A4s, and Stanier's Princess Royals and Princess Coronations respectively: one followed the other in a quickfire Thirties technological evolution. The streamlined Princess Coronations were often called 'Big Lizzies' as a nod to their immediate predecessor.

The Princess Coronation tenders were equipped with a steam-operated coal pusher to bring the coal down to the firing plate, enabling firemen to meet the high demands for power during the non-stop run of 299 miles between Euston and Carlisle on the 'Royal Scot' bound for Glasgow Central.

The first five Princess Coronations,

Sir William Stanier, who brought his vast locomotive knowledge acquired from working for the GWR on the King and Castle classes to the LMS.

A contemporary hand-coloured view of LMS Princess Coronation Pacific No. 6220 *Coronation* leaving London for Crewe with the 'Coronation Scot' preview run on June 29, 1937 that would claim a 114mph British steam record. The newer No. 6229 *Duchess of Hamilton* would take this locomotive's identity for its transatlantic trip to New York's World Fair in 1939-40. ROBIN JONES COLLECTION

This Lancashire & Yorkshire Railway dynamometer car was used to test LMS locomotives such as the Royal Scot, Princess Royal and Coronation classes. Built in 1912 and first numbered 293, after the Grouping it became LMS No. 45050. Withdrawn in 1967, it is now preserved in the Princess Royal Class Locomotive Trust's West Shed home at the Midland Railway-Butterley in Derbyshire. ROBIN JONES

Nos. 6220-4, all of which were allocated to Camden shed, were fitted with a trademark bulbous art deco casing and painted Caledonian Railway blue with silver horizontal lines to match the 'Coronation Scot' train that they were built to haul.

The wheels, lining to the edges of the bands, and the background to the chromium-plated nameplates were painted in a darker blue.

The styling of the streamlined casing was influenced by German and American designs. However, as was the case with Gresley's A4s, critics have argued the casings of both had more to do with style rather than substance, and claimed it made no difference at speeds lower than 90mph.

Scale models of the Princess Coronations were tested in the wind tunnel at the LMS scientific research laboratory in Derby.

A model made to Coleman's design showed that the bulbous front end disturbed the air less than the A4's wedge, but the downside was that there would be less clearance of exhaust gases, and smoke would drift into the driver's line of vision.

SMASHING THE CROCKERY

Selected to drive No. 6220 *Coronation* on a preview run to reclaim the British record from the LNER was Tom Clark.

On Tuesday, June 29, 1937, with a press trip before the official launch of the 'Coronation Scot' a week later, No. 6220 covered the 158 miles from Euston to Crewe in two hours nine minutes 45secs, reclaiming the British record with a top speed of 114mph.

The 114mph, taken from the locomotive's speed indicator, was claimed just before milepost 156, south of Crewe, although some experts said that 113mph, the same as the LNER record at that time, was more probably the correct figure, as the speed indicator was not usually considered sufficiently accurate for detailed timings.

Seasoned observer Cecil J Allen was on board alongside other timing experts, and none recorded anything higher than 112.5mpm, at mileposts 155 and 156. However, it was considered possible that 113mph was reached in-between.

This outward trip ended with a hair-raising experience, when Clark did not allow adequate braking distance before the 20mph limit on a reverse curve approaching Crewe. The train was still travelling at the top speed, with spectators from the town gathering on the lineside. Clark applied the brakes, but the train sped on with flames leaping from the brake blocks.

No. 6220 was travelling at 60-70mph when it approached the Crewe Platform 3 signal, he said.

Famously, crockery in the dining car was sent crashing before Clark slowed down to around 60mph and then 52mph on the first of three reverse curves on a trackwork complex with a series of crossovers. Standing passengers were flung off their feet, although none were injured apart from bruising, and a few of the rail chairs were also damaged.

Yet Clark still brought the train to a standstill at Crewe, with the locomotive and all of the carriages still on the rails. He proved that both the Princess Coronation and the permanent way could handle it. The overall time from Euston was 129.75mins at an average speed of 73.1mph, with the final 1.1 miles to Crewe station achieved in one minute 19secs. The return trip from Crewe back to Euston took 119mins, an average of 79.7mph, one of the fastest-ever recorded in Britain. The train arrived back at Euston early, having cut 16mins off the journey, and the LMS immediately claimed the fastest start-to-stop runs over 100 and 150 miles.

On July 12, 1937, two weeks after the record run, Tom Clark was presented by King George VI with an OBE. However, by then the fate of the crockery at Crewe led to the rivals agreeing to call a halt to risky record-breaking trips being staged as PR stunts.

Sporting the LMS crimson lake livery that the real No. 6220 *Coronation* never carried, Princess Coronation Pacific No. 6229 *Duchess of Hamilton* masquerades as the class doyen, with its 'Coronation' train, at the New York World's Fair. COLOUR-RAIL

CHANGING PLACES

Coronation may have stolen the headlines, but a sister locomotive took its place, and identity, for a prestigious transatlantic trip.

No. 6229 *Duchess of Hamilton* was built at Crewe in 1938 as the 10th member of its class and became "No. 6220 Coronation" – along with a complete 'Coronation Scot' train comprising three articulated pairs of coaches, a sleeping car as well as a club car, and represented the LMS at the New York World's Fair in 1939-40.

It was not the first time that the LMS had sent a locomotive with another's identity to the USA. In 1933 No. 6152 *The Kings Dragoon Guardsman* was sent to the Century of Progress International Exposition in Chicago as class doyen No. 6100 *Royal Scot*, and kept that identity after it returned to the UK.

For the World's Fair, No. 6229 was chosen because at the time it was the latest locomotive to come out of Crewe.

The central theme of the fair was the future, with an opening slogan of 'Dawn of a New Day', and it set out to showcase 'the world of tomorrow'. So the LMS decided to exhibit its most modern train to the rest of the world.

The identity exchange left a blue-liveried 'No. 6229 Duchess of Hamilton' running in Britain, and a crimson lake 'Coronation' in North America.

To comply with US railroad laws, 'No. 6220' was fitted with a huge headlamp and brass bell along with brackets for side-lamps and a claw coupling. None of the other LMS streamliners ever had such features.

The tour train ran from Crewe to Euston where it was publicly unveiled on January 9, 1939. The train including 'Coronation' was hauled from Willesden to Southampton Docks and loaded aboard the Norwegian *MV Belpamela* which was specially designed for shipping railway vehicles, and sailed on January 26. The ship arrived in Baltimore on February 20.

The train was unloaded four days later, and taken to the Baltimore & Ohio Railroad's workshops at Mount Clare for the locomotive to be reassembled.

A private test run was followed by an unveiling to a VIP audience in the workshops on March 17, with a press run to Washington and back the next day.

The train first made a 3121-mile tour of the USA, hosted by the Baltimore & Ohio Railroad, as a build-up to the World's Fair.

It began on March 21, with the starting signal being electrically activated directly from the fairground.

The tour was a massive success, with the 'Coronation' aka *Duchess of Hamilton* attracting crowds wherever it went. It was estimated that around 425,000 people came on board at the stations to inspect the luxurious interior, and two million people saw it at the fair itself.

The grand opening of the fair took place on Sunday, April 30, the 150th anniversary of George Washington's inauguration as president in New York City. Albert Einstein gave a speech, in which he discussed cosmic rays, before the ceremonial lighting of the fair's lights.

Crowds flock to welcome 'No. 6220 *Coronation*' to Hartford, Connecticut. THE RAILWAY MAGAZINE

Princess Coronation Pacific No. 6229 *Duchess of Hamilton* as No. 6220 *Coronation* departs Hartford, Connecticut, on the New York, New Haven & Hartford Railroad during its US tour. THE RAILWAY MAGAZINE

Sister locomotive No. 6245 *City of London* was built in 1943 and became the first of the class to be painted in wartime unlined black livery, a fate that befell *Duchess of Hamilton* after it returned from the USA. THE RAILWAY MAGAZINE.

DEFYING THE U-BOATS

There would be no quick homecoming for the pseudo-*Coronation*. The outbreak of the Second World War in September 1939 led to shipping cargoes being restricted to food and military supplies.

The World's Fair organisers asked for 'Coronation' to be exhibited for another year, and the LMS was left with no option but to agree.

However, despite the shipping losses incurred during the German U-boat offensive in the Atlantic, by 1942 the LMS was suffering a shortage of locomotives and took the view that the need for another Pacific outweighed the risks of seeing it end up at the bottom of the Atlantic.

Loaded on to the *SS Pioneer* it arrived back safely at Queen Alexandra Dock in Cardiff on February 16, 1942, and was hauled via Shrewsbury to Crewe. It re-entered service as No. 6220 *Coronation*, minus the US headlamp and bell. A year

No. 46229 *Duchess of Hamilton* in BR maroon heads through Ashton on April 24, 1962. K FAIREY/COLOUR RAIL

later it went back to being No. 6229 *Duchess of Hamilton* again, when both engines were in for repair at Crewe.

Back as No. 6229, it remained at Crewe North shed until the end of the year before being transferred to Camden, where it stayed until 1947.

The 'Coronation Scot' carriages came back in 1946, but by then, the 'Coronation Scot' was no more.

No. 6229 *Duchess of Hamilton* was painted into wartime unlined black livery in November 1944. Like other members of its high-profile class, its streamlined casing was removed in December 1947 for maintenance-efficiency reasons and it

was then given the LMS 1946 black livery. In 1948 it passed into British Railways ownership, with 40000 added to its number to become No. 46229 on April 15 that year.

Duchess of Hamilton was painted in the short-lived BR express passenger blue livery in April 1950, and April 26, 1952 it was repainted again, this time into Brunswick green.

The semi-streamlined smokebox, which had facilitated the streamlined casing, was replaced with a round-topped version in February 1957, and in September 1958, No. 46229 was painted maroon.

HI DE HI!

Only one Princess Coronation Pacific was officially preserved for the nation, and that was No. 46235 *City of Birmingham*. Mainly because of its name, the city council offered to display it inside its extended Museum of Science & Industry.

Reading enthusiast Brian Walker tried in 1963 to drum up support among local authorities for classic LMS locomotives to be saved, but interest proved sparse, at first.

He wrote to holiday camp magnate Billy Butlin, successfully asking for help for the funds that had been set up for No. 46201 *Princess Elizabeth* and No. 46100 *Royal Scot*, suggesting that a place for saved locomotives might be found in the holiday camps.

Butlin's then decided to buy locomotives from British Railways itself and asked about the availability No. 46220 *Coronation* for its Minehead camp, because of its historic US trip. However, Brian Walker pointed out that No. 6229 had been the locomotive that crossed the Atlantic, not the real No. 6220.

Butlin's therefore chose No. 46229 and *Duchess of Hamilton* was duly taken to Crewe Works for cosmetic restoration.

On April 24, 1964, it was moved south by rail to Minehead and towed up the branch line to the West Somerset resort behind GWR 0-6-0 pannier tank No. 9647, which did not survive into preservation.

Butlin's displayed No. 46229 at Minehead from April 1964, and camp staff did their best to look after it, regularly greasing moving parts and applying aluminium paint to rods and motion, which helped delay corrosion. Yet they could not hold back the corrosion caused by the salt-laden Bristol Channel air.

As the Crewe paint job began to fade, and interest among the young campers slowly died following the end of British Railways' main line steam, what had been a star attraction became an eyesore.

By 1970, Butlin's began looking for new homes for the steam locomotives.

Eventually, the Science Museum and Butlin's agreed a 20-year lease of No. 46229, which would see it restored cosmetically at Swindon Works, and then transferred to the new National Railway Museum at York.

The Minehead branch was closed by British Rail in 1970, but the track was

No. 46229 *Duchess of Hamilton* as a static exhibit at Butlin's holiday camp in Minehead. It was displayed next to London, Brighton & South Coast Railway 'Terrier' 0-6-0T No. 32678 *Knowle*, which later returned to steam on the Kent & East Sussex Railway. ROBIN WEBSTER*

left in place because of plans to reopen it as the West Somerset Railway. It was decided to take No. 46229 out by the way it had arrived, by rail, and in March 1975, a low loader took it from the holiday camp top nearby Minehead station before it was towed to Taunton and on to Swindon Works.

It was decided to restore *Duchess of Hamilton* in its final BR condition, and the smoke deflectors, which had not been displayed at Minehead, were replaced. No. 46229 was unveiled at the new York museum on May 26, 1976, at a dinner held to mark the centenary of Stanier's birth.

LMS Princess Coronation Pacific No. 46229 *Duchess of Hamilton* passes Cross Gates with BR's 'Scarborough Spa Express' on August 16, 1984. BRIAN SHARPE

BACK ON THE MAIN LINE

LMS expert and author, the late David Jenkinson, a member of the museum's curatorial staff in the mid-Seventies, suggested that money should be raised to return *Duchess of Hamilton* to steam. At the time, there were no other examples of the class – two others had survived into preservation – in running order.

The slow overhaul of the Duchess began in May 1978, and on May 1, 1980, it undertook a trial run.

Nine days later, No. 46229 hauled two trains around the York-Leeds-Harrogate circle under the banner of the 'Limited Edition'. It joined the Rocket 150 cavalcade on May 24-26 the year, celebrating the 150th anniversary of the Liverpool & Manchester Railway.

On November 1, 1980, the Duchess made its eagerly awaited heritage-era debut on the Settle to Carlisle line, but stalled in bad weather on the climb past Stainforth, and needed assistance from the rear by Class 40 No. 40134.

On May 23, 1981, No. 46229 hauled the first 'Scarborough Spa Express' which was scheduled to run on summer Tuesdays and Wednesdays from York to the resort and back, following an agreement between the Eastern Region and Scarborough Borough Council, which saw a 60ft turntable from Gateshead installed at Scarborough, with financial assistance from the local authority.

Hugely popular with the public, No. 46229 became a mainstay of steam motive power on the main line, at one stage being temporarily based at

Marylebone, and running over routes that were new to the class. However, on October 26, 1985, it made a farewell trip with the 'Cumbrian Mountain Express' before its seven-year main line boiler ticket expired.

During its six years back on the network. No. 46229 covered a total of 13,223 miles.

A second overhaul, costing the Friends £220,000, saw extensive work on the boiler carried out and a new tender tank made, increasing the water capacity by 1000 gallons by eliminating the space for two tons of coal.

However, the electrification of the East Coast Main Line saw the cab height lowered. New cab side sheets were fabricated and the safety valves had to be reduced in height. The end result was a locomotive that stood 13ft 1in above rail level, giving adequate clearance.

In 1987, the museum bought No. 46229 outright from Butlin's and at last it became part of the National Collection.

No. 46229 resteamed on December 9, 1989 at a special day for supporters at the York museum.

The locomotive ran light engine from Derby for weighting and adjustment

No. 462239 *Duchess of Hamilton* at the Rocket 150 event at Rainhill in 1980. BARRY LEWIS*

of springs on March 28, 1990, and successfully undertook a loaded test run to Sheffield the following day, after which a new main line certificate was awarded.

On Good Friday, April 13, 1990, *Duchess of Hamilton* returned to service hauling a Pullman train on a 280-mile return trip from York to Carlisle over the Settle and Carlisle line.

However, BR announced that No. 46229 had to be diesel-towed between York and Leeds.

As No. 47555 *The Commonwealth Spirit* towed No. 46229 and train under Holgate Bridge at the south end of York station, its comeback seemed pointless.

In July 1991, *Duchess of Hamilton* returned to the North Wales Coast line. A season based at Crewe Heritage Centre resulted in trips to Llandudno and Holyhead, to Shrewsbury and Hereford and the infamous 'Red Rose' around Lancashire.

The purpose of that trip was to get locomotives from Crewe to Carnforth without using the obvious route, as steam was not then allowed to go direct.

New ground for the class was covered towards the end of 1992 when the Friends chartered a train from York to Workington via Leeds and Carnforth, while early 1993 saw No. 46229 back on the Settle and Carlisle route.

'FIFTEEN GUINEA SPECIAL' RERUN

To celebrate 25 years since the end of steam an attempt was made to re-run the landmark 1T57 'Fifteen Guinea Special' on August 11 that year. Gradually, by the time all the rearrangements had taken place, it became a super-version of the 'Cumbrian Mountain Express' from Leeds, with Duchess power!

Of course No. 46229 had been withdrawn five years before the end of steam, but Britannia Pacific No. 70013 *Oliver Cromwell*, which had run on that last day in 1968, was not available. In its place, No. 46229 performed faultlessly and the passengers were left very happy.

However, they were less happy on the 'Cumbrian Mountain Express' run of September 18.

The Duchess had just left Bradford when it was obvious that all was not well. Finally it came to a halt at Bell Busk. The silence that befell the whole train was such that you could hear a pin drop.

Duchess of Hamilton at the former Steamtown museum at Carnforth on April 10, 1982. BRIAN SHARPE

Green swansong: a storming performance from green-liveried *Duchess of Hamilton* during an otherwise dull and overcast February 25, 1998. FRED KERR

No. 46229 had not failed on a train since its return to steam in 1990 but this was serious. Eventually Class 47 D1962 (which was following to take the train back from Carlisle) buffered on at the rear and pushed the whole ensemble to Hellifield. There No. 46229 was placed in a siding and the train went north behind D1962.

The problem was a hot bearing and so No. 46229 had to return to York light engine at reduced speed overnight.

On August 28, 1994 the Friends chartered the Duchess to run an echo of the much-lamented 'Scarborough Spa Express.' At the time, with British Rail having gone into serious death throes during privatisation, it proved very difficult to arrange this train. Two straightforward runs from York to Scarborough should have been fairly simple. But it was anything but.

The stock, from Manchester, courtesy of Regional Railways, arrived late. From then on it seemed as if the train was there under sufferance.

The trip gave the Friends such a bad experience that it was the last time the group chartered a full train. Nevertheless No. 46229 performed faultlessly and appetites were whetted for some longer runs again. On December 17, a southbound 'Cumbrian Mountain Express' helped get No. 46229 back in the swing.

Crewe and York were the main line operating bases for No. 46229 during 1995 after which a spell at the East Lancashire Railway in return for maintenance saw an interesting return to York. On March 30, 1996, No. 46229 hauled an ELR-sponsored train from Preston to Manchester Victoria, then via Standedge and Healey Mills to York and Scarborough. On the return the locomotive went back to its base at York.

October 19, 1996 was the day that No. 46229 returned to Shap. Heading a Days Out railtour from Crewe to Carlisle

and back, it was the first time it had hauled a train over the northern part of the LNWR main line since 1963.

Racing through Carnforth, where unique BR 8P Pacific No. 71000 *Duke of Gloucester* was on hand to give a supportive whistle, the Duchess was soon hard at work climbing the Lakeland fells. Roaring up to Dillicar, a temporary restriction resulted in a slackening of speed to Tebay. Then it was on to the final slog.

From passing Tebay, speed increased for some time before the gradient began to bite back. The crowds waiting to see the train go past were not disappointed as No. 46229 mounted the summit at 57mph.

That year saw No. 46229's final main line run, heading the 'Royal Scot,' a Days Out trip, which took in the entire West Coast Main Line from Euston to Glasgow on November 30, and then the East Coast route from Glasgow to York on December 1. It was on this journey that No. 46229 gained its reputation as the fastest British steam locomotive in preservation at that time.

Its main line ticket having expired, and restricted to heritage lines, the following months saw No. 46229 visit the Mid Hants, the Nene Valley and the East Lancashire railways. At the latter, it was agreed that No. 46229 could be painted in BR Brunswick green for enthusiast photographic charters as long as it was repainted in crimson before being returned to York.

Its final day in service was March 21, 1998, when on one run it double-headed with LNER A4 Pacific No. 60007 *Sir Nigel Gresley*, an inconceivable combination in the days of steam but one with immense novelty value for those who travelled. Withdrawn at the peak of performance, it was intended to overhaul No. 46229 back to operational condition, but financing of the work never materialised.

Duchess of Hamilton's last public appearance in its destreamlined condition was at the Great Gathering: Crewe Works open weekend on September 10-11, 2005.

The streamlined tender with fins fitted at the rear. ROBIN JONES

RECREATING ART DECO GLORY

Duchess of Hamilton's foreseeable future lay as a static exhibit. However, there were murmurings afoot about going one better, and giving it back its original streamlined casing.

During 1998, talks between the National Railway Museum and Steve McColl, production director of luxury train operator Venice Simplon Orient-Express, and the former head of British Rail's Special Trains Unit, about rebuilding Duchess of Hamilton in its original form and returning it to the main line were conducted. To cut a long story short, they came to nothing.

In early 2002, Bury locomotive engineer and owner Ian Riley asked the museum if he could restore Duchess of Hamilton to its original streamlined condition for main line running, but again, the subsequent talks bore no fruit.

However, in 2004, the museum announced that it was to spend £70,000 on a fresh study into the feasibility of restreamlining No. 46229, in partnership with the Friends of the NRM's 229 Club and Tyseley Locomotive Works in south Birmingham.

A museum spokesman said: "This is a unique project not only because of the nature of the task, but also because many of the skills used in Crewe works to complete the locomotive will have

The streamlined casing around the front bufferbeam, and the platform to support the two front doors of the housing, as seen on May 26, 2007. ROBIN JONES

been lost and the study will seek to rediscover exactly how the streamlining was constructed and applied to the locomotive. This is also the condition in which the engine toured the United States before the outbreak of the Second World War."

The 229 Club unanimously approved the scheme, with father-and-son team Bob and Alastair Meanley overseeing the engineering at Tyseley Locomotive Works.

The following year, Duchess of Hamilton appeared as a static exhibit at the Great Gathering: Crewe Works Festival of Rail open weekend on September 10-11, after which it was hauled by diesel to Tyseley. A study showed that restreamlining was feasible, and the museum gave the go-ahead. A nationwide appeal to fund the project was launched, and raised around £30,000, to which the Friends of the NRM added another £60,000.

However, it became clear that another £20,000 was needed. Bob Meanley, Tyseley's Chief Mechanical Engineer brought in an outside contractor to bend the metal sheet to construct the front doors of the casing because of their extremely complex geometrical shape.

Paint manufacturer John Scanlon of Weston-super-Mare supplied the paint for the project free of charge, and it was matched to the exact shade of the original LMS crimson with gold lining.

Paint changes colour over time, so there was no easy way of knowing exactly what shade of LMS red or maroon Duchess of Hamilton was painted in when it was outshopped in 1938.

However, painter Bob Timmins, had taken part in a debate over the colour of 'LMS red' back in the Sixties, during which he met a man who had a barrel of LMS red dried powder pigment.

This man gave Bob Timmins a bag of the pigment, which afterwards remained

perfectly preserved in the darkness of his attic for more than 40 years.

At Tyseley, Duchess of Hamilton was fitted with a new tapered smokebox to accommodate the casing.

Before the streamlined casing could be formed, the correct steel needed to be found. A worldwide search led to a year-long stalling of the project.

A year into the search, Corus, Europe's second largest steel producer, was able to roll steel of the correct size and thickness especially for the project. Several sheets of the 1.5mm steel sheet were obtained with the aid of former Prime Minister Gordon Brown's office.

Furthermore, the locomotive's cab was found to be out of position and in need of rectification work.

Finally, the Duchess was towed back to the York museum on May 18, 2009, behind a diesel, all set for its high-profile public relaunch.

The casing in place inside Tyseley Locomotive Works on January 21, 2009. ROBIN JONES

Old rivals meet at last: May 17, 2013, saw *Duchess of Hamilton* lined up alongside a Gresley A4, the temporarily repatriated No. 4489 *Dominion of Canada*, on the apron outside the Locomotion museum at Shildon. ANTHONY COULLS

A STREAMLINED DUCHESS BACK AFTER 60 YEARS

On the evening of May 20 VIPs turned out to see the 'new' No. 6229 make its debut in the museum's Great Hall. There was nothing but praise for the end result.

The last time a Princess Coronation Pacific in its original streamlined form had been seen was in 1949, when No. 6243 *City of Lancaster* had its air-smoothed casing removed.

The 'reborn' No. 6229 immediately became the subject of a new exhibition, Streamlined: Styling An Era, which explored the links between Thirties society, engineering and art deco design using the Duchess as the central exhibit.

Museum display content manager, Joe Savage, said: "*Duchess of Hamilton* is a stunning example of art deco opulence, which when it was built in 1938, wowed design critics on both sides of the Atlantic. Its streamlined look was symbolic of the trend, which became the icon of an era.

"It is one of the most significant products of the streamline era. Its streamlined form embodied the language of speed and sold an exciting image of modernity to potential passengers.

"During a time of hardship the streamlined shape turned *Duchess of Hamilton* into an exciting symbol of progress and now, even in the current economic climate; it still has the power

to inspire." In early 2011, the National Railway Museum's then director Steve Davies raised the possibility of a future return of *Duchess of Hamilton* to steam and the national network.

In the meantime, for static display purposes, the museum repainted one of its LMS coaches, a corridor third-class brake, into streamlined LMS crimson lake with gold speed lines to match No. 6229.

Will *Duchess of Hamilton* ever run again, streamlined or not? It remains a perennial question, and no doubt more schemes will be thrown into the melting pot.

If it ever happens, it would be simply magnificent.

Even the headlamps are art deco. ROBIN JONES

LEFT: Bob Meanley, Chief Mechanical Engineer at Tyseley Locomotive Works, who masterminded the implementation of the restreamlining project. ROBIN JONES

The epitome of transport design in the art deco era: the air-smoothed casing of *Duchess of Hamilton* is mirrored by the curves of this fabulous Chrysler Airflow C1 from 1935, which was displayed alongside the Stanier masterpiece during and after its relaunch at the National Railway Museum on May 20, 2009. The Airflow was one of the first full-size American production cars to use streamlining as a basis for building a sleeker automobile, one less susceptible to air resistance. Despite its striking appearance, the Airflow proved a huge commercial failure. ROBIN JONES

The National Collection's LMS Corridor Brake Third No. 5987 as repainted in crimson lake livery with gold speed lines to match *Duchess of Hamilton*, is now permanently displayed behind the iconic locomotive in the Great Hall of the National Railway Museum. ROBIN JONES

GREEN ARROW

Grounded by its monobloc

After *Flying Scotsman*, Gresley V2 2-6-2 No. 4771 *Green Arrow* has been one of the most popular LNER performers in the heritage era. Yet its future now lies as a static exhibit because of a historic problem that bested many members of the class.

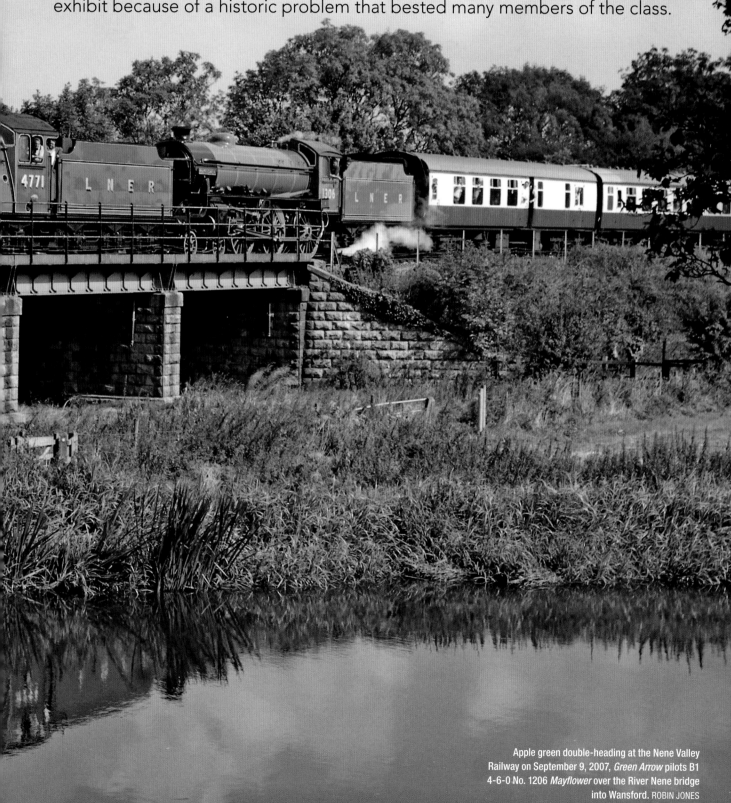

Apple green double-heading at the Nene Valley Railway on September 9, 2007, *Green Arrow* pilots B1 4-6-0 No. 1206 *Mayflower* over the River Nene bridge into Wansford. ROBIN JONES

Gresley V2 2-6-2 No. 4771 *Green Arrow* takes part in the Rocket 150 event at Rainhill 150 in 1980. BARRY LEWIS*

Nigel Gresley's V2s were the LNER's most famous mixed-traffic design, and one of his most successful locomotive types.

The design originated in 1932 when a modification of the K3 2-6-0 was being considered, including a rear bogie, which was shared with the tender and would have created a 2-6-4-4, unique in British railways. Within a year, however, the articulated tender was abandoned to give a 2-6-2 arrangement that allowed the classic Gresley wide firebox to be fitted.

By 1934, the proposed design was streamlined with the proposed new locomotive essentially a 2-6-2 version of P2 2-8-2 *Cock o' the North*, and a Kylchap exhaust, rotary-cam poppet valve gear, and ACFI feed water heater.

Ultimately, these, as well as the streamlining, were discarded at the drawing board stage in favour of a conventional appearance.

The first five V2s, Nos. 4771-75, were ordered in May 1935 and appeared in 1936, with a double-beat type regulator, which Gresley had adopted from French practice. The cylinders, steam chests, and various passages were housed in one large monobloc casting, which saved weight and cut the risk of potentially leaky flange joints.

A total of 184 V2s in 11 batches was built between 1936 and 1944. The only major class of 2-6-2 tender locomotives used in Britain, they were allocated to all regions of the LNER, but were predominantly used along the East Coast Main Line between King's Cross, Edinburgh and Aberdeen, occasionally substituting for the A1 and A3 Pacifics and even the streamlined A4s. However, because of their 22-ton axle load, their use was restricted to around 40% of the LNER's route miles. They could not use the former GER main lines because of their weight.

The first of the class, No. 4771 *Green Arrow* quickly became famous working the first leg of the King's Cross to Glasgow express goods.

The V2s really came in to their own during the Second World War, when they hauled numerous heavy passenger trains, many with more than 20 carriages loaded to 700 tons. On one occasion, a V2 hauled 26 coaches from Peterborough to King's Cross.

Gresley recognised that a lighter mixed-traffic locomotive was needed for wider use, and his V4s were designed to this end. Yet it was his successor, Thompson, who finally plugged the gap in the fleet, with his far more numerous B1 4-6-0, which replaced the V2 as the LNER's standard mixed-traffic locomotive.

The railway network suffered badly from lack of maintenance during the war, and in 1946, several accidents involving V2s becoming derailed were blamed on a combination of the poor condition of the track, and Gresley's double swing-link pony truck design. Accordingly, the V2s were converted to a less-sensitive pony truck design, that used by the Thompson L1s. After several V2s suffered monobloc cracks, a modified design was introduced in January 1942, moving the upper flanges to ease maintenance. When production ceased in 1944, the V2s were the last Gresley engines being produced.

Despite this innovation, by the mid-1950s, maintenance of the monoblocs was becoming too expensive. If one cylinder cracked, the whole monobloc would have to be replaced.

In May 1956, BR introduced a new policy whereby if one cylinder needed to be replaced, the monobloc was replaced with three separate cylinder castings. A total of 71 V2s lost their monobloc castings in this way.

In the early Sixties, trials with double blastpipe/chimney arrangements borrowed from the LMS Royal Scot class led to some improvement in economy, though not to the extent experienced with the Kylchap system on the A3 and A4 Pacifics.

Nevertheless eight V2s were converted to use the Kylchap double chimney arrangement before the class was inevitably superseded by diesels, withdrawals beginning in February 1962.

By that December, 69 V2s had been withdrawn, and the last in service was York's No. 60831 and Dundee's No. 60836, which lasted until December 6, 1966, when they became the last of Gresley's big engines to be withdrawn.

LIFE AS A HERITAGE-ERA ICON

As the first of the class, *Green Arrow* had already been preserved as a part of the National Collection, having been withdrawn from service on August 21, 1962.

No. 4771 had been based at King's Cross throughout its working life, apart from a six-week period from May 1953 when it was temporarily allocated to Woodford Halse on the former Great Central Railway's London Extension. Indeed, the class were regular and popular performers on the GCR main line.

In its first decade in preservation, *Green Arrow* was externally restored at Doncaster Works to LNER apple green livery and appeared destined for a museum in the town. When this project failed to materialise No. 4771 was placed in store, along with other engines at Hellifield shed. A move to Leicester followed, where there was another proposal for a museum, but again Green Arrow escaped incarceration as those plans were downsized and the engine went back into storage, this time at

Green Arrow on display inside the Locomotion museum at Shildon. GILLETT'S CROSSING*

OVERHAULED FOR ANOTHER DECADE

Green Arrow ceased to run in 1987 when boiler leaks were discovered. However, to the rescue this time came Huddersfield industrialist, Dr Michael Peagram, who provided £100,000 sponsorship. The V2 duly returned to steam on August 12, 1998.

Green Arrow returned to the Great Central Railway at Loughborough twice in 2000, including a starring role in the inauguration of the railway's double track. Visits to heritage lines by the V2 had been unknown in its earlier preservation career, but the National Railway Museum

was now more relaxed about letting it stay away for periods on loan. Its main line operations also extended their scope, with the V2 travelling as far afield as Holyhead, Cornwall and Weymouth, turning in superb performances on unfamiliar routes such as the South Devon banks.

On February 1, 2003, *Green Arrow* finally made it back 'home' to King's Cross, with Past-Time Rail's 'Dick Turpin' tour from York.

The V2s carried LNER apple green livery when new, but most were black

during the war, reverting to apple green afterwards. As mixed-traffic engines, BR painted them in lined black, until 1957, when the class joined several other types in qualifying for the passenger livery of Brunswick green, so *Green Arrow* was once again green. It carried its BR livery as No. 60800 for several years in preservation. However, for what turned out to be the final two years of heritage-era running, No. 60800 once again reverted to the apple green No. 4771, the repaint being carried out by Wabtec at Doncaster Works.

LNER V2 2-6-2 No. 4771 *Green Arrow* crosses Ais Gill viaduct on the Settle and Carlisle line on September 30, 1989. BRIAN SHARPE

LNER V2 2-6-2 No. 4771 *Green Arrow* at Wansford station on the Nene Valley Railway on September 9, 2007. BRIAN SHARPE

Preston Park, Brighton.

No. 4771 was finally 'rescued' from obscurity by former Norwich shedmaster Bill Harvey. The Norfolk Railway Society restored it to main line operating condition in 1973, following the lifting of the BR steam ban the previous year.

Main line runs followed, mainly from Tyseley and Carnforth, on the very limited routes available to steam in the Seventies.

In 1975, *Green Arrow* took part in the Rail 150 cavalcade at Shildon to mark the 150th anniversary of the opening the Stockton & Darlington Railway and moved to the then-new National Railway Museum in York, where it was in steam for the opening ceremony performed by the Duke of Edinburgh on September 27 that year.

The V2 quickly established itself as a favourite at the museum, and was frequently seen on main line runs to and from the city, but it rarely stayed away for more than a day or two, and remained on display when not on main line duties.

One of the defining moments of steam preservation came in March 1978 when, after a gap of 10 years, steam returned

to the Settle and Carlisle route. David Ward, in his role as passenger marketing manager for the London Midland region, permitted the return of steam to the line after a decade's absence, *Green Arrow* was the chosen engine, heading north on Easter Saturday, returning on the Monday.

No. 4771 clocked up 10 years of quite intensive main line use, though rarely straying from the north of England, and when the boiler certificate expired, there was hardly a second thought about overhauling the engine and carrying on as before. The work was carried out by the Humberside Locomotive Preservation Group at Hull, under the leadership of Tom Tighe, and when the V2 returned to the main line, its options were now a little wider.

Steam had returned to London on a regular basis, and *Green Arrow* ventured to Marylebone, the former Great Central terminus, which had been a regular haunt of V2s in days gone by.

THE MONOBLOC PROBLEM
Towards the end of steam, BR had decided against replacing any further

V2 monobloc castings and by the early 1960s, if they were worn, then the engine was withdrawn. *Green Arrow* was a relatively early withdrawal and being one of the unconverted engines, it could be assumed that its monobloc casting was well-worn.

It had always been an area that its custodians have kept a close eye on, and although it had not been covering the mileages it would have covered in regular service, *Green Arrow* had run for longer in the heritage era than it did in LNER/BR days, so its major component, already known to be worn, was clearly not getting any better.

The deteriorating condition of *Green Arrow* gave many cause for concern, not least of all the NRM, which in May 2007, announced that it would be withdrawn from the main line, after a routine boiler inspection revealed a degree of wear to the firebox foundation ring studs, which was felt to be unacceptable to sustain the 75mph performance required to operate on the national network.

However, it was agreed that *Green Arrow* would still fulfil its obligations to heritage lines, and proposed visits to the

Gloucester Warwickshire, Nene Valley, Severn Valley, East Lancashire and Churnet Valley railways went ahead.

No. 4771's last engagement was appropriately on an LNER route, the North Yorkshire Moors Railway, where it was be matched with a set of Gresley teak-liveried coaches, for its last few weeks of service. After announcing a full programme of farewell runs, including two weekends of the line's LNER gala, on April 1, 2009 No. 4771 succumbed to leaking superheater elements… but then came the final surprise trip.

Moves behind the scenes had begun to enable Gresley V2 2-6-2 No 4771 *Green Arrow* to see out the end of its boiler ticket.

Grosmont engineers made a full assessment of the situation and approached the museum with an action plan to carry out a temporary repair to allow one of the most popular preservation icons of all time to make one last return trip over the Moors line on Saturday, April 26.

The plan was accepted, and the locomotive department staff set to work, pulling out all the stops to make the trip happen, albeit with the V2 running at yet further reduced boiler pressure, along with the museum proviso that it was banked all the way, by LNWR 'Super D' 0-8-0 No. 49395.

As it happened, it ran one-and-a-half round trips, departing Grosmont to Pickering with an empty stock train – the NYMR's Gresley teak set, of course – at 10.30am, in top-and-tail mode with the 'Super D'.

Facing south, it was on the back of

Green Arrow undergoing maintenance in the National Railway Museum's workshops in York in November 2005. ROBIN JONES

the noon departure from Pickering to Grosmont, which arrived shortly after 1pm. It then departed Grosmont at 1.30pm and arrived back into Pickering at 2.45pm, the trip costing £25 per head, and limited to 80 seats on a first-come, first-served basis. In addition to the public, museum staff members of the NRM travelled to say their farewells to 'a much-loved friend'.

Afterwards, the V2 stayed behind at Pickering, where its last fire was thrown out before it was taken away by low loader, to start what appears to be an indefinite sojourn at Locomotion: The National Railway Museum in Shildon.

NYMR general manager, Philip Benham,

said: "We were delighted to be able to offer the public a last chance ride, especially after the disappointment of the mechanical failure three weeks before."

The big problem is the V2's unique monobloc cylinder casting, which needs to be replaced. The NRM has so far backed away from replacing the cracked monobloc as it is an historic component, though it could be stored for posterity or placed on display while a replacement keeps the locomotive running.

So, unless there is a change of heart or a major sponsor comes forward, one of our most-loved performers of the heritage era will remain silent for the foreseeable future.

V2 No. 60800 *Green Arrow* departs from Bodmin Parkway with a service to Bodmin General in May 1999. At the time it was the biggest steam locomotive to have visited the Bodmin & Wenford Railway. ROBIN JONES

Chapter 20

THE Q1
Back to basics and beyond

In the wake of the 2008 banking crash, which set off a global recession, every day we hear politicians talk about 'austerity' measures.

Yet austerity is nothing new, and during the Second World War, it impacted on British locomotive design.

Engineer Robert Riddles designed Austerity 2-8-0s and 2-10-0s for the War Department, and 494 examples of Hunslet's Austerity 0-6-0ST were built by several different manufacturers, many bound for military services.

Yet in appearance Southern Railway Chief Mechanical Engineer Oliver Bulleid's Q1 heavy freight 0-6-0s pushed the concept to its limits.

As a child, I used to think of these locomotives with their unmistakeable unique design as sets of dustbins on wheels. As far as cosmetic appearance was concerned, the Q1s were the other

Q1 No. C1 as it appeared in a maker's photograph in 1942, when the heavy freight class first appeared. THE RAILWAY MAGAZINE

end of the scale from Bulleid's air-smoothed Pacifics. Yet they helped Britain win the Second World War.

The Q1s lacked elegance and refinement and had no airs and graces, yet they were unstoppable workhorses for which few tasks were too great.

With war on the horizon, the Southern Railway had an urgent need for a new no-holds-barred freight locomotive, and Bulleid knew that once hostilities broke out, there would be a colossal expansion of goods traffic in south-east England, which would become a front line in the defence of the realm from a Nazi-occupied Europe. Yet the Southern Railway had instead invested in third-rail electrification of lines in the area.

The most modern freight locomotive to the SR was Richard Maunsell's Q 0-6-0s, last design for the Southern Railway, and the company's first own 0-6-0 design, They replaced ageing pre-Grouping 0-6-0 goods classes, which had remained to serve on various secondary routes and branches from which heavier and more powerful engines were barred. While the Qs first appeared in 1938, their design originated in late Victorian time.

Suddenly, more freight locomotives

52/363 BUILT BY 1954
JOHN BOYD & CO (ENGRS) LTD
ANNAN SCOTLAND

were needed, ones with a high tractive effort capable of hauling the heaviest troop and military supply trains.

Hailed as the ultimate development of the British 0-6-0 freight engine, Bulleid's 40 Q1s were capable of hauling trains that were normally allocated by other Big Four companies to much bigger types.

Their unconventional appearance earned them such names as Biscuit Tins, Biscuit Barrels, Charlies Clockworks, Coffee Pots, Frankensteins and Ugly Ducklings.

Bulleid, who replaced Maunsell in late 1937, took into account the impending wartime austerity regime and incorporated the minimum amount of raw materials, removing all unnecessary cosmetic features and any running plate and splasher, and came up with the most powerful 0-6-0 ever to run in Britain. Weight-saving principles came to the forefront: because a Q1 weighed less than 90 tons, it could be used over more than 97% of the Southern routes, so that ugly minimalist design played a big part.

Exerting 30,000 lb at 85% boiler pressure, the Q1s had at 27sq ft, the largest fire grate area of any British 0-6-0, weighing 14 tons less than a comparable engine. Also, their cylindrical shape allowed them to be driven through a coach washer for cleaning at a time when manpower could not be spared.

Furthermore, the lagging was provided by Ideglass, a glass fibre insulation material that was cheap and plentiful during the war years. However, it could not support any weight, and therefore a separate casing was required, and as with the Merchant Navy Pacifics, the boiler rings were adapted to lend the lagging the support needed.

Q1 0-6-0 No. C1 stands on the turntable in the Great Hall on April 23, 2017. ROBIN JONES

The boiler design was based on the Lord Nelson class, and the firebox used the same throatplate and backplate. The first batch of 20 Q1s was built at Brighton Works, appearing in 1942, and the second 20 at Ashford.

Mainly freight engines, they were sometimes used on passenger trains on secondary routes.

After peace was declared, the Q1s had many more years of service to come as British Rail gave them the power classification 5F.

Withdrawals began in 1963, as a result of modernisation, and Nos. 33006, 33020 and 33027 were the last in service in 1966. However, because of the huge and successful role that the class played in the war, it had decided to save the first Q1, No. 33001, for the National Collection following its withdrawal in 1964.

It spent much time in preservation working on the Bluebell Railway in the home territory for the class. However, after working on the heritage line for 27 years (during which time it was overhauled twice), after its boiler ticket expired, with no prospect of a fast-track overhaul in the workshops, in 2004 it was taken to the National Railway Museum at York where it remains on display in the Great Hall. Its running days are not necessarily over, for it might one day return to the Bluebell Railway.

BELOW: Painted in Southern Railway livery as No. C1, the first of Bulleid's 'Ugly Duckling' Q1s, No. 33001 has a starkly contrasting appearance to other locomotives in the Great Hall at the National Railway Museum at York. ROBIN JONES

Again carrying a headcode mirroring the wartime Prime Minister' V's for Victory salute, No. 34051 *Winston Churchill* stands at the head of the recreated funeral train inside the Great Hall of the National Railway Museum on the morning of January 30, 2015. Its entrance into the museum at 8am lit the touchpaper for a series of national celebrations marking the 50th anniversary of Churchill's funeral train. ROBIN JONES

V for Victory!

Entirely deserving of a place in the National Collection purely because of its name and the funeral train that it hauled more than half a century ago is Bulleid Battle of Britain Pacific No. 34051 *Winston Churchill*.

IT was not only the LNER that ran streamlined Pacifics. The Southern Railway had its own fleet too, designed by Oliver Vaughan Snell Bulleid – who was Nigel Gresley's assistant when he produced the A4s.

There were three different variations of Bulleid Pacific – the Merchant Navy 4-6-2s and their lighter counterparts the West Country and Battle of Britain classes. Thirty Bulleid Pacifics survived into preservation, and examples of all three classes can be seen in action in Britain today, not only on the main line but on heritage railways too.

However, only one of those made it into the National Collection, and for its name alone, never mind any other curatorial considerations, it was one that could never have been refused. No. 34051 *Winston Churchill*.

The coat of arms carried by No. 34051 *Winston Churchill*. ROBIN JONES

WINSTON CHURCHILL
BATTLE OF BRITAIN CLASS

No. 34051 at the head of the funeral train on January 30, 1965. MIKE EVANS

Bulleid was interviewed by Southern Railway general manager, Sir Herbert Walker, on May 11, 1937, and he went on to take over the position of Chief Mechanical Engineer on October 1 that year. Now the SR had arguably one of the best CMEs in the country, a man with first-hand knowledge of Gresley Pacifics, with their free-steaming boilers and fast three-cylinder layout.

In 1938, Bulleid was given the go-ahead by Walker's successor as general manager, Gilbert Szlumper, to produce designs for 20 express passenger locomotives.

Bulleid took the same stance as Gresley had done when he designed the A4s. His aim was to produce a superior and modern steam locomotive that would be a genuine alternative to diesel and electric traction, not just stop gaps until the inevitable and steam was withdrawn en masse.

He came up with a new Pacific, one that would be equally at home on express and semi-fast services, with Bulleid building on his first-hand expert knowledge of the Gresley types.

The SR's plan for a Pacific fleet of its own was stalled somewhat, but not derailed, by the outbreak of the Second World War as armaments and munitions production by necessity took priority.

Bulleid's first streamlined Merchant Navy Pacific, No. 21C1 *Channel Packet*, emerged from Eastleigh on February 18, 1941, and was officially named at a ceremony at Eastleigh Works on March 10, by the then minister for transport, Lt-Col JTC Moore-Brabazon.

Its streamlined shape was as distinctive as that of the A4s, but its main purpose was not aerodynamics, as evidenced by the extremely flat front end, but smoke deflection. In this and several

other aspects, Bulleid's Pacifics diverged from Gresley's. The flat sides were also an aid to cleaning the locomotive with a carriage washer, in a bid to reduce labour costs.

Bulleid had long since come to the conclusion that it was far better not to have working parts exposed to the elements where they ended up being plastered by dirt thrown up from the track. He also took the view that steam engines should get nearer to the internal combustion engine, which enclosed the working parts and used pump lubrication to keep it all running smoothly.

While the streamlined casings of the A4s earned them the nicknames of 'Streaks', Bulleid's Pacifics became known as 'spam cans'.

To countermand the weight problem with the Merchant Navies, Bulleid came up with a lighter version. No. 21C101 *Exeter*, the first of the Battle of Britain class and West Country class light Pacifics, made its debut in 1945, and eventually a total of 110 of both classes were built.

Bulleid Pacifics were the flagship in the south and south-west of England until the end of steam on the Southern Region in 1967, hauling famous named trains such as the 'Atlantic Coast Express'. Indeed, the final British Railways' steam train into Waterloo was the Weymouth boat express hauled by Merchant Navy No. 35030 *Elder Dempster Lines* on July 9, 1967.

The Battle of Britain Pacifics were given names after places and heroes connected with the UK's darkest hour and, in the circumstances, greatest triumph.Continental influence came to the fore when Bulleid introduced a new numbering scheme to the SR. Letters and numbers were used to designate the

powered and unpowered axles, and so a Pacific – a 4-6-2 – became 21C1, with C referring to the three driving axles, 2 to the number of powered axles and 1 to the unpowered axles.

A GREAT BULLEID FOR THE GREATEST BRITON!

Battle of Britain Pacific No. 21C151 was built at Brighton Works in 1946, and released to traffic on December 30 that year. It was first allocated to Salisbury shed for services on the West of England Main Line between London and Exeter.

No. 21C151 was officially named *Winston Churchill* in a ceremony at Waterloo station on September 11, 1947. The former prime minister, by then leader of the opposition, was offered the chance to name the locomotive, but turned it down, claiming a prior engagement.

The locomotive was named by Lord Dowding, who also named his own locomotive, No. 34052, at the same ceremony. Churchill became the only person to decline the opportunity to name a Battle of Britain class locomotive after himself. In October 1948, following Nationalisation No. 21C151 received its British Railways' number, 34051.

It also kept its Southern Railway malachite green with chrome yellow striping until November 1950 when it was repainted into BR Brunswick green.

In February 1950, No. 34051 moved to Nine Elms locomotive shed in London, and continued to work the West of England Main Line, as well as the Waterloo to Weymouth line. In April 1951 it was reallocated to Exmouth Junction shed, and transferred to Salisbury only two months later. It stayed there for the rest of its career, becoming the shed's 'pet' locomotive.

BRITAIN'S SADDEST HOUR

Winston Churchill died on January 24, 1965, at the age of 91. His state funeral took place in St Paul's cathedral six days later and a train to carry his coffin also took world leaders from Waterloo to Handborough station in Oxfordshire, the nearest station to the village of Bladon where he had wished to be buried in the parish church close to his family's ancestral seat of Blenheim Palace.

There was only one choice of locomotive to haul that train. No. 34051 *Winston Churchill*.

Besides No. 34051, the train comprised Southern Region gangwayed bogie luggage van No. S2464S, which had been specially converted into a hearse van, in Pullman cream and umber colours to match the coaches in the train; Pullman guard parlour cars No. 208 and *Isle of Thanet*; kitchen parlour cars *Carina*, *Lydia* and *Perseus*. Indeed, in anticipation of Churchill's death, the luggage van had been withdrawn from normal service in 1961, and was set aside and repainted into the Pullman colours in July 1962. It was kept out of public gaze in Stewarts Lane carriage sheds. Until then, it had been a mere regular goods van carrying vegetables and newspapers.

Three headcode discs on No. 34051 were arranged in a unique V formation, recalling Churchill's famous Victory sign. There was was one disc on each side of the smokebox, and a third in the middle of the bufferbeam. Under normal circumstances, that headcode would have been used only for a breakdown train. Following the service at St Paul's, the coffin was taken up the River Thames on *MV Havengore* before being transferred to Waterloo station.

The train was routed via Twickensham, Ascot, Wokingham and Reading, where it left the Southern Region and joined the Western Region. It ran via Didcot East and North junctions as well as Oxford before stopping at Hanborough, which was decorated in white and purple drapes, and from where the coffin and mourners were taken to Bladon by road.

It was the last steam-hauled state funeral train in history.

No. 34051 then retraced its route back to London light engine, the special train being taken back to Paddington by Western diesel-hydraulic

D1015 *Western Champion*.

No. 34051 was withdrawn on September 19, 1965, having covered 807,496 miles.

Onlooker David Monk-Steel, from York, then a keen trainspotter who worked as a clerk in an engineers' office in 1965, joined the crowds of people gathering on the platform at Clapham Junction to see the funeral train pass by.

He recalled: "British Transport Police were in attendance but they did not seek to chase us away so we settled in to wait.

"The first sign of the occasion was the passing of No. 34064 *Fighter Command*, all 'bulled up'. This was the stand-by locomotive running ahead of the special.

"Then the special itself came into view. The locomotive had three discs on the front in a 'V' formation, which I later discovered usually indicated a breakdown crane going to clear the line! On this occasion it signified Churchill's 'V' for victory hand gesture…

"I tried to capture a couple of pictures with my Kodak 127 camera, a cheap and cheerful contraption that took only eight frames, and was, for me, on my lowly clerk's wages an expensive luxury."

NRM interpretation developer, Jamie Taylor, said: "Churchill's funeral was watched by 300 million people on television worldwide and his last solemn journey by train has really stuck in people's memories."

Sir Winston Churchill and Dwight D Eisenhower, Supreme Commander of the Allied Expeditionary Forces in Europe. Churchill was the only leader who declined to personally name a locomotive after himself.

SAVED FOR THE NATION HE SAVED

After the funeral train, No. 34051 was then set for preservation, and in November that year, it was stored at Hellifield, later being displayed at Didcot Railway Centre.

It was later moved to the National Railway Museum at York, where it is on display today. However, it has never steamed in preservation. There would be little commercial sense in returning it to steam, because, as stated, there are already several sister locomotives in operation today.

With the 50th anniversary of the death of the great wartime leader on the horizon, the Friends of the National Railway Museum launched an appeal to give the locomotive a facelift in January 2011.

The Mid Hants Railway's Ropley Works was chosen to do the job, the repainting being completed in December 2014 after which the engine was returned to York for display in the museum in time for the 50th anniversary of the death of Winston Churchill the following month.

Hearse van No. S2464S, on loan from the Swanage Railway Trust, underwent restoration at the Locomotion museum in Shildon, during which, the outline of the markings for the resting place of the coffin was rediscovered.

Sir Winston Churchill's funeral train passing Clapham Junction; the second carriage is the hearse van. BEN BROOKSBANK*

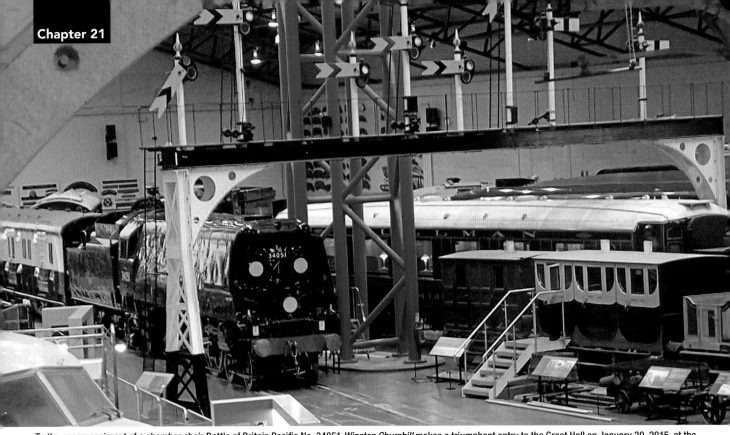

To the accompaniment of a chamber choir Battle of Britain Pacific No. 34051 *Winston Churchill* makes a triumphant entry to the Great Hall on January 30, 2015, at the head of a train that included two vehicles from the funeral train it hauled 50 years to the day before. ROBIN JONES

WE WILL NEVER FORGET

AT 8am on Friday, January 30, a whistle was sounded as a train was shunted into the Great Hall of the York museum to choral accompaniment.

As a crowd of VIPs, from across Britain fell silent, the beautifully refurbished No. 34051 entered in front of a rake of two vehicles, which had also formed part of its namesake's state funeral train exactly 50 years before.

Then came Pullman car No. 246 *Lydia*, which had, during the Second World War, formed part of Churchill's command train.

The entry of the recreated funeral train into the museum kicked off a series of nationwide commemorative events including a flotilla down the Thames including the barge that had carried Churchill's coffin in 1965, alongside the stretch where, famously, the dockyard cranes bowed their jobs in respect as it passed by.

As with the train that ran half a century before the three headcode discs were arranged in the unique 'V' formation.

The funeral train remained on display in the Great Hall until May 2015, as the centrepiece of an exhibition that recalled

the part the railway played in the only state funeral granted to a statesman in the 20th century.

The accompanying display included archive news footage of the funeral, which saw the crowds throng the lineside through Churchill's final journey, while millions more worldwide clustered around their TV sets to bid farewell to the man who had saved Europe and much of the rest of the globe from the tyranny of an evil ideology.

However, the star of the show this time round was Jim Lester, 72, the fireman on the footplate of No. 34051 on

Pullman carriage *Lydia* was manufactured by the Birmingham Carriage & Wagon Company in 1925. It was significantly damaged when it was struck by an excursion train just outside Leeds Central station in 1959, but was repaired at Preston Park works for a grand total of £820. Stranded in the USA after Alan Pegler's *Flying Scotsman* tour of North America went bust in 1969, in 2000 it was repatriated to the UK along with sister car No. 247 *Isle of Thanet*, which also featured in the funeral train. Owned by enthusiast David Westcott, the pair were restored and stored at West Coast Railway's Carnforth base, pending an eventual move to the Swanage Railway once a carriage shed became available. Interior table lamps for the funeral train exhibition were provided by the Pullman Society. ROBIN JONES

Jim Lester, the fireman on the funeral train 50 years previously, reunited with No. 34051 inside the National Railway Museum on January 30, 2015. ROBIN JONES

The Southern Region van that was repainted into Pullman colours in anticipation of it being used to haul Churchill's funeral train. ROBIN JONES

RIGHT: The interior of the baggage car where the coffin was laid. ROBIN JONES

that historic journey half a century ago. Jim, whose railway career began in 1957 as a cleaner at Nine Elms and finished in 2004 as the traction officer at Eurostar, said: "It's been great working with the museum on this display to mark this anniversary and for me; it's like turning the clock back 50 years.

"I'm a little more hard of hearing than I was back then but the sound of that whistle and seeing the locomotive and train, together again, has brought it all back to me, the huge crowds watching us go past and the deep sense of sadness that was evident on the occasion.

"The steam days were always special to me, and my journey on the funeral train stands out in particular. My memories remain with me today."

Also present was Steve Davies, the former NRM director who asked for No. 34051 to be restored because of its deteriorating condition.

Anthony Coulls, the NRM's senior curator of rail vehicles, said: "Our locomotive and the carriages that it hauled have earned a place on the national stage due to the part they played in Churchill's final journey. Until they were chosen to take the statesman on his

final farewell, they were just standard rolling stock, especially the baggage van, which carried everyday goods before it was selected to transport Churchill's coffin."

Also justifiably given pride of place were the team from Ropley Works, which carried out the meticulous cosmetic restoration of No. 34051, after it had been found that not only had the paintwork faded but much of the 'spam can' casing had rotted away from the inside, and their counterparts at Locomotion museum in Shildon who had restored the baggage car.

On January 30, from the footplate of No. 34051, National Railway Museum director, Paul Kirkman, officially opens the funeral train exhibition watched by Philip Benham, chairman of the museum's Friends group. ROBIN JONES

Bathed in sunshine as well as glory. No. 34051 *Winston Churchill* stands inside the Great Hall of the National Railway Museum on January 30, 2015. ROBIN JONES

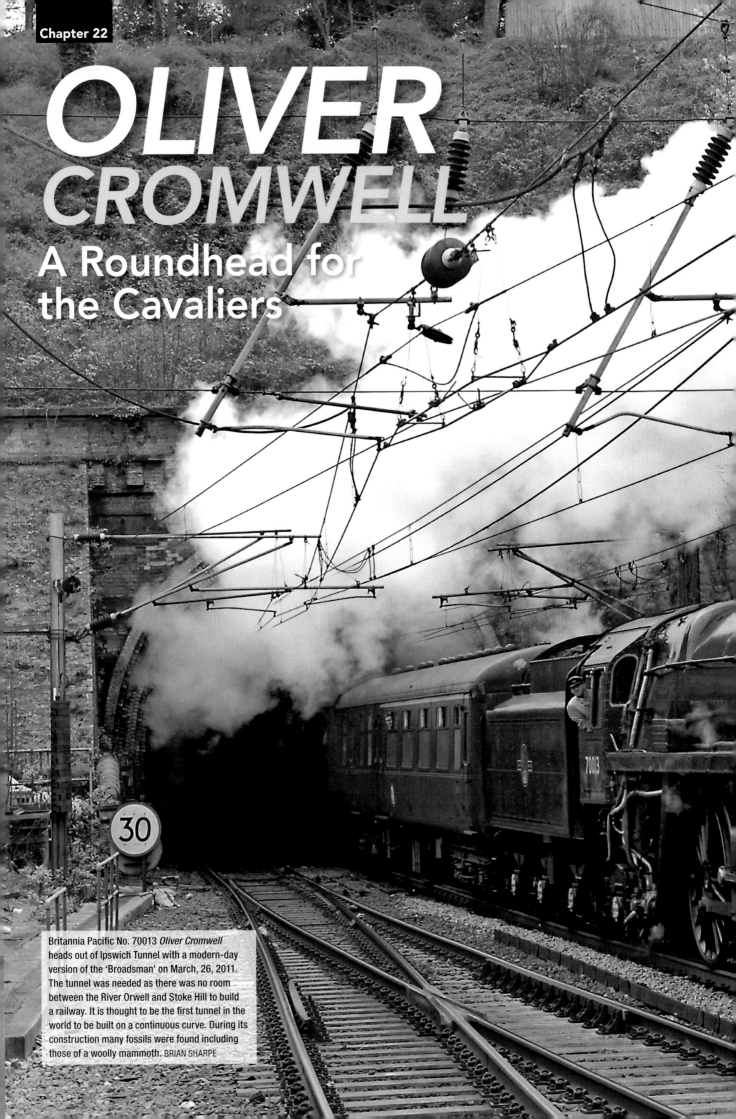

OLIVER CROMWELL

A Roundhead for the Cavaliers

Britannia Pacific No. 70013 *Oliver Cromwell* heads out of Ipswich Tunnel with a modern-day version of the 'Broadsman' on March, 26, 2011. The tunnel was needed as there was no room between the River Orwell and Stoke Hill to build a railway. It is thought to be the first tunnel in the world to be built on a continuous curve. During its construction many fossils were found including those of a woolly mammoth. BRIAN SHARPE

After it hauled British Rail's last steam special, the 'Fifteen Guinea Special' on August 11, 1968, Britannia Pacific No. 70013 was officially preserved, but squirrelled away in a museum. It did not haul another passenger train for four decades, until it was overhauled to working order on the Great Central Railway.

Following Nationalisation in 1948, in the years of postwar austerity, British Railways could not afford to follow the lead set by other countries such as the United States in eliminating steam in favour of diesel and electric traction.

That would come eventually, but for now steam had to suffice. If that was to be the case, there was a need for new steam locomotives to replace aging Big Four and pre-Grouping locomotives still in service.

Robert Riddles, who had been director of transportation equipment at the Ministry of Supply during the Second World War designing the WD Austerity 2-8-0s and WD Austerity 2-10-0 s, and who had been promoted to vice-president of the LMS in 1944, was appointed as a member of the Railway Executive for Mechanical and Electrical Engineering at Nationalisation. Under him, British Railways produced 12 Standard classes of steam locomotive to hold the fort before modernisation could take place.

The first BR Standard design to emerge was a Class 7 two-cylindered Pacific, designed at Derby in 1951. Nothing like it had ever been seen in Britain before.

There was little need for them except on the Great Eastern lines. A few went to the Western Region to supplement the Castles but the region generally hated them. Two, for internal BR political reasons, went to the Southern Region and worked the 'Golden Arrow' to Dover.

On these top-link duties, *Oliver Cromwell* moved to March but had little to do and moved on to the London Midland Region, which had a few spread around, while a handful went to Scotland.

In theory, if steam had lasted another 40 years, hundreds may have been produced and maybe they would have ultimately displaced Castles, Bulleid light Pacifics, Royal Scots and LNER V2s, reducing operating and maintenance costs, but it was never going to happen.

On August 11, 1968, *Oliver Cromwell* passes Ais Gill with IT57, the fabled 'Fifteen Guinea Special' which ended British Railways' main line steam haulage. ALAN BROWN

The new Class 7s had 6ft 2in driving wheels, following Bulleid's Pacifics and Peppercorn's LNER A2s, which had proved that this was no obstacle to high-speed performance.

The choice of the name Britannia for the first of the new Pacifics reflected the regard that Riddles felt for the LNWR where he had started his railway career, which had a locomotive running under that name. Also, No. 70000 *Britannia*

appeared in 1951, the year of the Festival of Britain.

The Britannias revolutionised the Great Eastern main line, but only for 10 years, and once they left East Anglia, they moved around various sheds gradually becoming concentrated on the LMR, where they became the last working British Pacifics, but they had ridiculously short lives on the front-line services they were designed for.

The class was concentrated on the Carlisle sheds in 1967 but their numbers steadily reduced and 13 were withdrawn on December 31 that year, leaving just one, transferred to Carnforth for special duties. No. 70013 *Oliver Cromwell*, named after the English Civil War leader.

The locomotive was built at Crewe in 1951 and was nothing special in itself, just another of the 55 Britannias, allocated along with 22 other class members to East Anglian expresses from Liverpool Street.

THE LAST TRIP OF THEM ALL

Once displaced from the LMR, it ended its days like many of the class working from Carlisle, although increasingly on freight work rather than passenger duties.

By 1967, the end of steam was in sight and one by one, the BR workshops ceased overhauling steam engines until only Crewe was still carrying out such work. No. 70013 was the last steam locomotive overhaul to be completed there and a small ceremony marked its outshopping on February 25, 1967 resplendent in fully lined green livery and even with a nameplate (on one side), to return to Carlisle for its last period of service.

Accordingly, No. 70013 was highly likely to end up being the last steam locomotive in BR service and did very little to justify the cost of this last

Who better to welcome *Oliver Cromwell* to the National Railway Museum than a platoon of Roundheads? Colonel Edward Montagu's Regiment of Foote, a Roundhead regiment of the English Civil War Society, is based around Leeds and Manchester, fires a welcoming volley at the 1968 And All That event on May 24, 2008. ROBIN JONES

overhaul, spending much of 1967 in store, while the two Carlisle sheds used their other Britannias, which were being gradually withdrawn when major work was required.

Oliver Cromwell was active towards the end of 1967 and had one last fling in real passenger duty, on a football special from Glasgow, which it worked from Carlisle to Blackpool on December 31, when the Carlisle sheds closed to steam and 13 Britannias were withdrawn and steam working ceased over both Shap and the Settle and Carlisle line.

However, No. 70013 was not withdrawn but was reallocated to Carnforth. It sat outside the shed foreman's office under a very tightly secured tarpaulin. In March, it emerged into the daylight and was steamed for a railtour, the first of many it would work in the period leading up to August that year.

Oliver Cromwell hauled a railtour marking the end of the Derby to Manchester main line in June and had a hectic few weeks of railtour operation leading up to August 11, even briefly seeing use on timetabled trains after some attention at Crewe works.

On August 11, it handled the Manchester Victoria to Carlisle leg of 1T57, the legendary 'Fifteen Guinea Special', BR's last standard gauge steam train.

David Greenhalgh, from Accrington, a fireman on part of the return run, recalled: "Roads were blocked with cars as the drivers had left them to catch a glimpse of this piece of history.

"It was as though a royal visitor was on board. Fortunately for everyone, it was a sunny day, but I guess the crowds would still have gathered had it been raining."

A NORFOLK SOJOURN

After that historic trip, *Oliver Cromwell* then ran light engine to Norwich and was transferred to Bressingham Gardens near Diss in Norfolk by road the following Sunday, destined not to haul a main line passenger train again for 40 years.

Up to 1973, however, it did at least give footplate rides on a short length of track at Bressingham, which had been successfully developed as a live steam museum by the late horticulturalist Alan Bloom.

The locomotive had been preserved and presumably officially, but that was only confirmed when No. 70000 *Britannia* itself was offered for sale by BR in 1969.

As the first in the class, it would normally have been the National Collection policy to preserve No. 70000. It was initially destined for official preservation because of its cultural significance, and was stored. However, partially owing to its prototype design and construction differences, and because No. 70013 has gone down in

Spring 2008 saw the National Railway Museum hold a nine-day event, 1968 *And All That*, remembering the end of steam haulage on the main line. No. 70013 *Oliver Cromwell* just had to be there, having pulled the 'Fifteen Guinea Special' the last BR steam special, and was joined by Standard 9F No. 92220 *Evening Star*, and GWR 4-6-0 No. 7029 *Clun Castle*, the last steam locomotive to haul a train out of Paddington. *Oliver Cromwell's* footplate was fully accessible to the public for the first time since completion of a four-year restoration project. ROBIN JONES

history as one of the last steam engines in BR service, the latter was chosen.

Britannia was eventually bought by Britannia Locomotive Company Ltd and returned to steam on the Severn Valley Railway before embarking on a glittering new career in preservation.

Once No. 70000 returned to steam in 1978, *Oliver Cromwell* was largely forgotten.

There were occasional calls to return *Oliver Cromwell* to the main line, notably in 1993 when Alan Bloom stood firm against a high-profile campaign to have it realised from Bressingham to head a 25th anniversary re-run of the 'Fifteen Guinea Special'.

He claimed that *Oliver Cromwell* had been placed there "on permanent loan" by the National Collection, and said that it was a key exhibit and its removal would lower the income from visitors to his venue.

He said he was prepared to release

it only if the National Railway Museum, which had assumed responsibility for all the National Collection locomotives from BR, would send a replacement exhibit of similar magnitude, and threatened to bar the gates if a low loader was sent to collect it.

The museum did not challenge the "permanent loan" claim, and No. 70013 stayed where it was.

Eventually, the NRM had to agree to Alan Bloom's apparently reasonable request that if the NRM wanted its engine, it had to loan him another one of equal status in its place.

This formed the basis of an agreement. The museum had too many engines to be able to display them and Bressingham had suitable secure covered accommodation, so the museum placed a couple more engines on loan so they could be on public view and added LNER V2 2-6-2 No. 60800 *Green Arrow* in steamable condition, to the mix.

Crowds gathered around the newly reinstated Station Road level crossing in Sheringham on as *Oliver Cromwell* heads 'The Broadsman', the first heritage-era incoming steam train from the main line on to the North Norfolk Railway, on March 11, 2010. ROBIN JONES

BACK IN ACTION AGAIN

No. 70013 finally left Bressingham by road on May 21, 2004. It was bound first for the Railfest 2004 event at the NRM at York, marking the bicentenary of Richard Trevithick's first public display of a steam locomotive on the Penydarren Tramroad near Merthyr Tydfil in 2004. Then it moved to Great Central Railway where it would be overhauled by a partnership of the Main Line Steam Trust, the Loughborough Standard Locomotives Group and the 5305 Locomotive Association, financed by a public appeal.

This team, in conjunction with the NRM, would manage and operate No. 70013 wherever it would run over its 10-year tour of duty. It was given a thorough overhaul and returned to GCR passenger service on May 3, 2008.

There was still the matter of the main line certification and time was tight but the engine made it to Carnforth and starred in an open weekend at West Coast Railways' base, which had been Cromwell's home shed for eight months in 1968. It worked a main line test train and duly took its place at the head of the 40th anniversary re-run of 1T57 on August 10, running once again from Manchester Victoria to Carlisle.

On September 9, 2008, *Oliver Cromwell* completed a re-run of 'The Norfolkman' running from Liverpool Street to Norwich and return, visiting the site of its former home of Norwich shed (32A). No. 70013 carried a 32A shed plate on the smokebox to complete the image.

November 8, 2008, the locomotive was temporarily renumbered as No. 70048 and renamed *The Territorial Army 1908-2008* to commemorate the 100th anniversary of the Territorial Army. The naming was performed by the Duke of Gloucester at Quorn & Woodhouse station on the GCR.

No. 70048, a sister locomotive, was named The *Territorial Army 1908-1958*. During the 2008 renaming, 70013 carried this name on the right-hand-side smoke deflector as a reminder of the original name and as a link with the past association of the Territorial Army.

On March 14, 2009 *Oliver Cromwell* hauled a special, which formed the last train over the Folkestone Harbour branch. The locomotive has since operated a many railtours in various parts of the country, including East Anglia and the North-West, in between spells working GCR services.

A major highlight was hauling 'The Broadsman' from King's Cross to Norwich, Sheringham and on to Holt over the North Norfolk Railway on March 11, 2010, the first passenger train to run over the reinstated connection between

LEFT: *Oliver Cromwell* heads under Kinchley Lane bridge on July 17, 2016, after returning to service on the Great Central Railway. ROBIN JONES

The Down 'Broadsman' pulled by No. 70013 *Oliver Cromwell* passes through Stratford in April 1958. BEN BROOKSBANK

A journey that started at Liverpool Street ended at the north Norfolk Railway's Holt station. *Oliver Cromwell* comes face to face with GER N7 0-6-2T No. 69621 on March 11, 2010. ROBIN JONES

Network Rail and the NNR.

Here was heritage-era history in the making. Pop mogul and railway enthusiast Pete Waterman was there to lead the cheers and gasps as No. 70013 hauled five carriages slowly across the tramway-style crossing on Station Road to mark the culmination of a £140,000 overhaul. Announcing the approach of the train, from a vantage point aboard an open-top bus, he simply said: "Here he comes. This is it - 46 years of waiting. Let's hear it for *Oliver Cromwell*."

On May 15, 2010, two years after its previous overhaul, *Oliver Cromwell* suffered from cracks in the firebox and was moved to the GCR for an inspection, which led to the locomotive being withdrawn from service. It underwent firebox repairs at Crewe Heritage Centre, and made its comeback on March 12, 2011, hauling 'The Lincoln Imp' from London Victoria to Lincoln, returning to King's Cross.

On May 27, 2012 the locomotive was involved in a blowback incident near Wood Green in North London on a Railway Touring Company railtour called 'The Peak Forester'. Two of the three crew members on board the locomotive attended hospital as a result.

On August 11, 2013 it worked the 'Fifteen Guinea Special' to celebrate the 45th anniversary of the ending of steam haulage on BR. This time round, No. 70013 was in charge of the Longsight to Carlisle leg of the special with the other legs being worked by 'LMS Black Fives' Nos. 45305, 45231 and 44932.

Early in 2015, after its appearance at the GCR's January gala, the National Collection engine was 'stopped' for substantial winter maintenance at Loughborough.

Work on the 'Brit' started with the replacement of a number of tubes, and ongoing work saw it withdrawn from main line duties.

However, it returned to GCR action over the weekend of July 16-17, 2016 after being laid up for 18 months and is now set for its main line comeback.

It was subsequently taken to the Midland Railway-Butterley to continue its intermediate maintenance programme, the main part of which was fitting new tyres from South Africa.

Once re-wheeled, it was returned to the GCR where the bogie set received attention at Loughborough courtesy of custodians the 5305 Locomotive Association.

It was subsequently laid up for repairs to its superheater elements and was due to make its latest main line comeback in 2017.

No. 70013 runs round its train at Loughborough Central station on July 17, 2016. ROBIN JONES

END OF THE LINE

BR Standard 9F 2-10-0 No. 92220 *Evening Star* was outshopped from Swindon Works in 1960, thus becoming the last steam locomotive built by British Railways and as such immortalised in legend. It was also the only British Railways' Standard locomotive earmarked for preservation that found its way into the National Collection.

While *Flying Scotsman*, the world's most famous locomotive, has so few original parts left that it may be considered more of a historical entity than a full-blown artefact, officials at the National Railway Museum point to BR Standard 9F 2-10-0 No. 92220 *Evening Star* as the most complete steam engine in the National Collection.

Outshopped from Swindon Works in March 1960, *Evening Star* is not only the newest main line steam locomotive in the collection, but the last of all to be built by British Railways. With only five years in traffic before it was made redundant by dieselisation, very few original parts would have needed to have been serviced or replaced.

The 9F 2-10-0 has been widely praised as the most successful of all the 12 British Railways' Standard types – yet whether they should have been built at all in the face of impending dieselisation remains questionable.

Although the design was shared between Brighton and Doncaster in 1953, the 251 2-10-0s were built at Crewe and Swindon, and allocated to the ER, NER and LMR at first, with the last batches going to the WR. Externally similar to a Britannia Pacific, the actual design was very different, with few parts common to both classes; in fact the 9F has surprisingly little in common with any of the other Standard classes, other than the external and relatively superficial cab, tender, footplating and smoke deflectors.

It was the last in the series of the BR Standard classes, and was intended for use on fast, heavy freight trains over long distances. BR was already planning increased use of continuous-braked 'block' freight trains but wagon and infrastructure construction would take time so the new heavy freight engine was a relatively low priority.

The Eastern Region's motive power officer, LP Parker, made the case for a new design of powerful freight locomotive, able to shift heavy loads at fast speeds in round trips between distant destinations within the eight-hour shift of the footplate crew.

BELOW: No. 92220 *Evening Star* passes Newbiggin with a southbound 'Cumbrian Mountain Express' on April 23, 1984. BSHARPE

Railway Executive mechanical engineer, Robert Riddles, took up the challenge, although ES Cox, supported by RC Bond, initially recommended a 2-8-2, Riddles was not convinced and having first convinced Cox, the decision was made on the 2-10-0 wheel arrangement for the increased traction and lower axle load that five-coupled axles can provide.

It was FG Carrier at Derby who had been largely responsible for the wartime Austerity 2-8-0s and 2-10-0s, who schemed out the 9F in mid-1951, but sadly did not live to see it. He proved that a wide shallow firebox with adequate ashpan capacity could be accommodated over 5ft-diameter coupled wheels. This

in itself is an obvious major difference between two apparently very similar Standard types as a 9F is not simply a 2-10-0 heavy-freight version of a Britannia; a Britannia boiler would never fit a 9F as the firebox had to be above a 5ft driving wheel, not a 3ft 3½in trailing wheel as on the Pacific. The initial thoughts of building a 2-8-2 version of a Britannia were that it could have utilised the same boiler.

The centre driving wheels of the 9F had no flanges, and those on the second and fourth coupled wheels were reduced in depth. This enabled the locomotive to round curves of only 400ft radius.

Riddles retired when the Railway Executive was abolished in 1953, and the first of his 9Fs appeared the following year. He became a director of a cranemakers in Bath, and died on June 18, 1983.

WHY BUILD STEAM AFTER BEGINNING DIESELISATION?

The following year, British Railways' Modernisation Plan was published, sounding the death knell for steam. In that case, why was a total of 251 9Fs built, at a time when diesel and electric traction had been publicly confirmed as the sole way forward?

The 9Fs were built with a life expectancy of up to 40 years, yet British Railways was to decree that steam haulage on the national network should cease in 1968.

No. 92210, for example, was therefore in service for just five years before withdrawal and scrapping, while No. 92004, which enjoyed the longest run, lasted 14 years. It is often claimed that the class was never given a real chance to show its true potential.

Compare and contrast the UK policy

of dieselisation with that of West Germany, where Pacifics ran alongside state-of-the-art diesels until the mid-Eighties.

Just as British Railways rushed into the diesel pilot schemes with mixed results, producing many unwanted types and wasting colossal amounts of public money, was the ending of steam as early as 1968 a point-of-principle move that saw perfectly serviceable modern locomotives scrapped with a few miles on the clock?

The cost of building a 9F rose by nearly 50% over the six years they were in production, from around £24,000 in 1954 to nearly £34,000.

While most of the 9Fs were built at Crewe, 43 of them were constructed at Swindon.

The first, No. 92000, emerged from Crewe in January 1954 and the initial eight were allocated to the Western Region for use on South Wales coal traffic.

The old Western hands did not like them at first and they experienced problems such as the steam brake being very slow to act after the locomotives had been standing, and a regulator which had the habit of sticking open. Complaints were such that the WR was not allocated any more until 1958, but nonetheless, the 9Fs proved very popular and successful elsewhere, especially on the Tyne Dock-Consett ore trains in the North East, as well as the Shotton steel trains in North Wales.

Apart from the War Department Austerity 2-10-0s built during the Second World War, the 9Fs were the only locomotive type with this wheel arrangement built for service in Britain.

Designed as no-nonsense heavy freight locomotives, they also saw occasional passenger service, including summer Saturday duties. A Swindon-built example, No. 92184 reached 90mph on Stoke Bank in Lincolnshire during one such turn on August 16, 1958 with the 14-coach Up 'Heart of Midlothian'.

THE BEST OF THE STANDARDS?

The 9F 2-10-0s were particularly successful. Although ideal for the slow heavy-freight haulage to be expected of Britain's most powerful steam engine, they were also capable of surprisingly fast running. The last batch went to the WR, which did not particularly want them but with no sufficiently powerful diesels available, 9F construction continued right up to 1960.

Although it was the planned change to high-speed 'block' freight trains that led to the building of the 9Fs, the process was even slower than anticipated and 9Fs tended to work slow, heavy unbraked freight trains throughout their careers, vindicating Riddles' choice of the 2-10-0 against the initial advice of Cox and Bond.

The 9Fs proved surprisingly suited to passenger work, capable of fast running despite their small driving wheels. *Evening Star* had a brief spell on Paddington-South Wales expresses and on one occasion on the East Coast Main Line, a 9F replaced a failed LNER Pacific at Grantham and headed an express to King's Cross, being recorded as exceeding 90mph.

However, this and other incidents prompted BR management to ban the class from express passenger work in view of the excessive wear and tear to the plain-bearing running gear.

The legendary Somerset & Dorset

BR Standard 9F 2-10-0 No. 92220 *Evening Star* outside the National Railway Museum on May 5, 2010. ROBIN JONES

Joint Railway main line between Bath Green Park and Bournemouth West famously saw 9Fs in service on passenger trains in its latter days.

The route over the Mendip Hills was notorious for its 1-in-50 gradients, which required double-heading, but one 9F could tackle them with ease – a huge bonus in the peak holiday season when crew numbers were low. Accordingly, four 9Fs were allocated to the route for several years.

Much was made by British Railways of the official naming of its final steam locomotive, 9F 2-10-0 No 92220 *Evening Star*, at Swindon on March 18, 1960. It would be Britain's last new main line steam locomotive until *Tornado* undertook its test trips in late 2008. COLOUR-RAIL

BRINGING THE CURTAIN DOWN

Swindon Works had the honour of building the last steam locomotive for use on the British main line, No. 92220 *Evening Star*, which was unveiled on March 18, 1960. When *Evening Star* rolled off the production line, it brought to an end a proud tradition of steam building at Swindon that had begun with the construction of Daniel Gooch's *Great Western* 114 years earlier.

The works made sure that the occasion would never be forgotten.

No. 92220, which cost £33,500 to build, was painted in passenger green livery (all other 9Fs were painted unlined black), its external pipe work made of copper and brass and its double chimney given a copper cap.

The name *Evening Star* was decided through a competition and was the choice of three Western Region workers: Mr Phillips, a driver based at Aberystwyth, Mr Pugh, a clerk in the general manager's office at Paddington; and Mr Sathi, a boiler washer at Old Oak Common. They realised that *Morning Star* was one of the first locomotives to run on the Great Western Railway, being supplied by Robert Stephenson before Daniel Gooch built his own, and so *Evening Star* would be a fitting finale to the steam age.

In a moving speech at the naming ceremony, proud Western Region chairman, Reggie Hanks, a former Swindon Works apprentice said: "There

No. 92220 on shed at Oxford in 1964. PETER ARMSTRONG*

had to be a last steam locomotive, and it is a tremendous thing that that last steam locomotive should be built here in these great works at Swindon.

"I am sure it has been truly said that no other product of man's mind has ever exercised such a compelling hold upon the public's imagination as the steam locomotive.

"No other machine in its day has been a more faithful friend to mankind nor has contributed more to the growth of industry in this the land of its birth and indeed throughout the whole world."

Evening Star was the only 9F to receive a name officially during its BR career.

Based on the Western Region, No. 92220 was not only in demand for enthusiasts' specials. It was closely controlled to ensure it returned home regularly for cleaning and maintenance, "in view of the special workings and

exhibitions for which the engine was required."

Evening Star also headed express workings to Paddington until it was banned from such high-speed duties (which it had coped with admirably). Cardiff Canton regularly used No. 92220 on the Up 'Red Dragon' express to Paddington. When the engine operated the 'Capitals United' express between Cardiff and London in July 1960, it also reached 90mph.

Evening Star, too, worked over the Somerset & Dorset line; it was chosen to haul the last of the route's most famous named train, the 'Pines Express' from Manchester to Bournemouth on September 8, 1962. After working from Oxford during the following winter, it even had a short period on the S&D the following summer but only on freight and local passenger work.

Hauling a rake of matching GWR-liveried coaches, in its final few months of operation, No. 92220 passes Castle Hill south of Williton on the West Somerset Railway on August 7, 1989. BRIAN SHARPE

LIFE AFTER BRITISH RAILWAYS

Evening Star was withdrawn after suffering front end damage in a collision and John Scholes, the curator of historical relics, refused to accept it and the WR would not repair it.

It was even briefly removed from the official list for the National Collection and offered for sale, but after storage at various locations in very poor condition it eventually found its way to Crewe Works where it was given a cosmetic restoration in 1967, apparently without any official authority from anyone.

However, it was then placed into storage at Preston Park in January 1968 along with other National Collection engines, which were awaiting a more permanent home where they could be displayed, although there was apparently still an interested purchaser for No. 92220.

At that time, there were already

thoughts of a new national railway museum and the 9F would eventually find a home there. In the meantime loaning National Collection engines to reputable preservation projects, steam centres and heritage lines was starting to gather pace and *Evening Star* was, in June 1973, loaned to the Keighley & Worth Valley Railway, one of the earliest steam heritage lines. It had shot to international stardom three years earlier when it was used for the location filming of the EMI big-screen production of Edith A Nesbit's classic, The Railway Children, starring Jenny Agutter.

Evening Star was steamed on arrival at the line and worked there during 1974-75 before making a triumphant comeback to the main line.

Its first heritage-era railtour saw it run Leeds to Grange-over-Sands and return on May 31, 1975. The locomotive was

transferred to the custody of the new National Railway Museum at York on August 31, that year.

It went on to operate railtours out of York, to Scarborough and over England's most scenic upland route, the Settle & Carlisle line.

Evening Star was loaned to the Great Western Society at Didcot on July 11, 1980 and overhauled, resteaming in September the following year and returning to York in May 1983.

No. 92220 worked railtours until September 1988, and then briefly worked on the West Somerset Railway, the former GWR Minehead branch and now at 24 miles Britain's longest independent steam line, from March 1989 until April 1990.

The locomotive returned to its Swindon birthplace in 1990, for static display, as part of that year's National Railway Museum On Tour exhibition. While the York museum was being refurbished, many items from the National Collection were displayed in Swindon Works.

Altogether nine members of the class survived into preservation, and five of these have operated at various times.

However, *Evening Star* is now on static display at the museum in York, with no plans afoot to return it to steam.

Owing to the 9F's flangeless centre driving wheels and the worry that the raised check rails on modern pointwork may cause a derailment, this class along with other 2-10-0s types, are presently banned from operating on Network Rail.

No. 92220 *Evening Star* at Bolton Percy on the Down Normanton line with the 8.23am York to Scarborough 'Scarborough Spa Express' on Sunday, August 14, 1983. DAVID INGHAM*

ABOVE: *Evening Star* pauses in York station with a 'Scarborough Spa Express' on August 14, 1983. BRIAN SHARPE

RIGHT: No. 92220 *Evening Star* at Rainhill during the Rocket 150 event in May 1980. GILLETT'S CROSSING*

No. 92220 at Haworth on the Keighley & Worth Valley Railway in September 1974. HUGH LLEWELYN*

Evening Star was not the last steam locomotive built in Britain during the steam era. That honour goes to reimported 1971-built Hunslet 0-4-0ST Trangkil No. 4, which is pictured visiting the National Railway Museum in May 2008. ROBIN JONES

RIGHT: *Evening Star* at the Great Central Railway's Leicester North terminus on May 20, 2015 – or was it? The National Railway Museum gave permission for sister No. 92214 to take on the identity of the real No. 92220. ROBIN JONES

NOT THE LAST
It is a common misconception that *Evening Star* was the last steam locomotive built in Britain. Not so: industrial standard gauge types continued to be turned out by Hunslet of Leeds in the early Sixties, along with narrow gauge locomotives for export and boilers.

Four years after *Evening Star* appeared, Hunslet built Britain's last all-new standard gauge steam locomotive, Austerity 0-6-0 saddle tank No. 3890. It was the last steam engine built for British use by a British manufacturer on traditional commercial terms.

The 484th Austerity 0-6-0ST to be constructed, it became No. 66 in the South Yorkshire NCB fleet and was sent to Cadeby Main Colliery, Conisbrough on March 27, 1964.

No. 66 was out of use at the colliery from 1970, after being replaced by a diesel, and several years later offered for sale. A member of Buckinghamshire Railway Centre beat off competition from 20 other potential buyers, including the NRM at York, to buy it. It was duly delivered to Quainton Road on November 4, 1975, and later became the property of centre operator, the Quainton Railway Society. It finally returned to steam in May 2015.

In 1971, Hunslet supplied an 0-4-0ST, works number 3902, from its Leeds factory to a sugar mill in Indonesia. It is held to be the last 'steam-age' locomotive built in Britain. This 2ft gauge locomotive, Trangkil No. 4 has since been reimported to Britain and restored to running order by enthusiast and modern-day narrow gauge locomotive builder, Graham Lee, for his private Statfold Barn Railway near Tamworth in Staffordshire, but for heritage rather than industrial use.

Of course, the building of new steam locomotives has never stopped in Britain, but these have all been for the enthusiast or tourist market, with model engineers' locomotives for miniature lines being at the lowest end of the scale.

However, in 2009, The A1 Steam Locomotive Trust saw the culmination of an 18-year project when new-build Peppercorn A1 Pacific No. 60163 *Tornado* made its passenger-hauling debut on the national network after undergoing tests in late 2008. It was the first steam locomotive built for the main line in the UK to enter traffic since *Evening Star* 49 years earlier.

WHEN 'EVENING STAR' STEAMED AGAIN
In 2015, 'Evening Star' was seen in action on the Great Central Railway.

The National Railway Museum agreed

No. 92220 *Evening Star* in the Great Hall of the National Railway Museum in April 2017. ROBIN JONES

Evening Star on display in STEAM – Museum of the Great Western Railway at Swindon. STEAM

for a sister locomotive to take its identity.

Loughborough-based No. 92214, which was bought by GCR supporter Cromwell Tools, after previously being based on the North Yorkshire Moors Railway, was painted in the same lined Brunswick green livery as carried by *Evening Star*.

It appeared in its new borrowed identity for the first time at the GCR's Railways at Work event on April 18-19 that year. New nameplates were made for No. 92214, together with other detailed features such as small brass plaques commemorating No. 92220 as BR's final steam locomotive.

Several photographic charters were arranged with the 'reborn' Evening Star, which would be in its element on the GCR double-track main line.

ANOTHER BRUNSWICK GREEN *EVENING STAR* ON THE MAIN LINE
In the 21st century, *Evening Star* did run again on the main line, in BR express passenger Brunswick green livery. However, there were no clouds of smoke.

For the *Evening Star* concerned was GB Railfreight's No. 66779, the last Class 66 diesel to be built for the UK and European markets.

The new Indiana-built *Evening Star* came face-to-face with the iconic Swindon-built No. 92220 – at its official naming ceremony at the National Railway Museum on May 10, 2016. The unveiling of its nameplate was conducted by Billy Ainsworth, chief executive officer of Progress Rail Services and Electro-Motive Diesel of Alabama.

Today's new locomotive is tomorrow's heritage, for GB Railfreight has said that it will donate the No. 66779 to the museum at the end of its working life.

Nose to nose: the *Evening Stars* of yesterday and today in the Great Hall of the National Railway Museum on May 10, 2016. BOB SWEET/GBRF

Catalogue of the National Collection

Here is a complete listing of all locomotives – steam, diesel and electric – that are part of the National Collection. The list is complete as of July 2017.

The oldest National Collection locomotive on display in the National Railway Museum at York is *Agenoria*, an 0-4-0 built in 1829 by Foster Rastrick and Company of Stourbridge. It first ran on June 2 that year along the three-mile Kingswinsford Railway linking mines in the Shutt End area of the Black Country with a canal basin at Ashwood on the Staffordshire & Worcestershire Canal. It is conjected that the locomotive ceased to run in the 1860s. After a period of neglect, the locomotive was rediscovered disassembled and covered with rubbish. One of its cylinders had been removed and used as a pumping engine. The person who rediscovered it, Mr EB Marten, obtained the permission of the owner, William Orme Foster, to reassemble the engine (including the missing cylinder) and display it at an exhibition in Wolverhampton in 1884. In December of that year it was presented to the Science Museum, which scrapped the tender. *Agenoria* was loaned to the LNER's museum at York in 1937 and also featured as an exhibit at the Festival of Britain in 1951. It is now on permanent display with a replica tender in the Great Hall. ROBIN JONES

LEFT: Visitors to the National Railway Museum at York come to see the biggest locomotives in the National Collection, but in the entrance foyer, they are greeted by one of the smallest. *Wren* is an 0-4-0ST built in 1887 for the 18in gauge internal system at the Lancashire & Yorkshire Railway's Horwich Works. It retired in 1962.

NATIONAL RAILWAY MUSEUM, YORK

LOCOMOTIVES

1829 Shutt End Colliery 0-4-0 *Agenoria*	(Great Hall)
1846 Furness Railway No. 3 *Coppernob*	(Great Hall)
1865 LNWR 0-4-0ST *Pet*	(Great Hall)
1869 NER 2-2-4T No.66 *Aerolite*	(Warehouse/paintshop)
1870 GNR 4-2-2 Stirling Single No. 1	(Great Hall)
(paired with 1893 GNR tender from Stirling Single No. 1002	(Great Hall)
1874 NER 0-6-0 No.1275	(Great Hall)
1874 Hebburn 0-4-0ST No. 2 *Bauxite*	(Great Hall)
1880 LBSCR 0-6-0T No. 82 *Boxhill*	(Learning platform)
1882 LBSCR 0-4-2 No.214 *Gladstone*	(Station Hall – Platform 1)
1887 L&YR 0-4-0ST *Wren*	(City entrance foyer)
1889 L&YR 2-4-2T No. 1008	(Great Hall)
1897 LSWR 0-4-4T No. 245	(Station Hall – Platform 6)
1898 GNR 4-4-2 No.990 *Henry Oakley*	(Great Hall)
1899 MR 4-2-2 No.673	(Station Hall – Platform 4/5)
1899 GNR 0-6-0ST No. 1247	(Station Hall – Platform 7)
1900 Hudswell Clarke 3ft gauge 0-4-0ST No.573 *Handyman*	(North Yard, mounted on BR machinery flat)
1901 SECR 4-4-0 No. 737	(Great Hall)
1905 4-4-2 Bassett-Lowke 15in gauge *Little Giant*	(Works Triangle)
1907 GWR 4-6-0 No.4003 *Lode Star*	(Great Hall)
1917 NSR Bo No.1	(Great Hall)
1923 LNER 4-6-2 No. 60103 (4472) *Flying Scotsman*	(Works for winter maintenance)
1926 LMS 'Crab' 2-6-0 No.13000	(Station Hall – Platform 2/3)
1934 L&MR 0-2-2 Rocket (sectioned replica)	(Great Hall)
1934 LMS 2-6-4T No. 2500	(Works)
1934 LMS 0-4-0DM No. 7050	(Station Hall – Platform 7)
1935 Chinese 4-8-4 No. KF7	(Great Hall)
1938 LNER A4 4-6-2 No. 4468 *Mallard*	(Great Hall)
1938 LMS 4-6-2 No. 6229 *Duchess of Hamilton*	(Great Hall)
1942 SR 0-6-0 Q1 class No.33001 (C1)	(Great Hall)
1949 BR (SR) 4-6-2 No. 35029 *Ellerman Lines* (sectioned)	(Great Hall)
1951 BR Bo+Bo No. 26020	(Great Hall)
1957 BR Bo-Bo Class 20 D8000	(Works)
1957 BR Class 31 No. 31018	(Great Hall)
1958 BR Class 40 D200	(Depot)
1960 BR 9F 2-10-0 No. 92220 *Evening Star*	(Great Hall)
1960 BR Class 37 D6700	(North Yard)
1960 BR Class 02 0-4-0DH D2860	(North Yard)
1961 BR Class 55 Deltic No. 55002 *King's Own Yorkshire Light Infantry*	(North Yard/Triangle)
1963 BR Class 52 D1023 *Western Fusilier*	(Works Triangle)
1965 BR Class 47 No. 47798 *Prince William*	(Works Triangle)
1973 BR Class 87 No.87001 *Stephenson/Royal Scot*	(Station Hall – Platform 6)
1979 L&MR 0-2-2 Rocket working replica	(Works)
1989 Hunslet Electric Adhesion Loco Mk2 ASDR1706	(Great Hall)

POWERED UNITS

1915 LMS (LNWR) motor open third brake No.28249	(Great Hall)
1925 SR 4-SUB motor third brake No. S8143S	(Great Hall)
1931 Post Office Railway underground train No. 809	(Great Hall)
1934 GWR AEC Railcar No.4	(Great Hall)
1976 West Japan Railways Shinkansen power car No. 22-141	(Great Hall)
1984 MAGLEV (Magnetic Levitation) Car ex-Birmingham Airport	(Works Triangle)
1992 BR Class 373/2 (Eurostar) power unit No. 3308 (E2014.0952)	(Great Hall)

LOCOMOTION - THE NATIONAL RAILWAY MUSEUM, AT SHILDON

LOCOMOTIVES

1829 L&MR 0-4-0 *Sans Pareil*

1837 South Hetton Colliery 2-2-2 *Bradyll/Nelson*

1840 S&DR Etherley tender only

1847 LNWR 2-2-2 No. 3020 *Cornwall*

1866 Stirling Goods tender (previously with Stirling Single

1892 LNWR 2-4-0 No. 790 *Hardwicke*

1893 NER 4-4-0 No.1621 (1975-7008)

1896 Sharp Stewart 4-8-0 3ft 6in gauge wood-burning locomotive No. 390 and tender

1898 W&C Bo No.75S

1902 GNR 4-4-2 No.251

1904 NER Bo-Bo No.1

1905 GWR 2-8-0 No.2818

1921 LNWR 0-8-0 'Super D' No. 49395

1925 Simplex petrol locomotive No. 4217

1935 LMS 4-6-0 No.5000 (1978-7040)

1936 LNER 2-6-2 No. 4771 *Green Arrow*

1946 BR (SR) 4-6-2 No. 34051 *Winston Churchill*

1953 BR Class 08 0-6-0DE No. 13079

1955 BR Class 55 Deltic prototype DP1

1956 Barclay fireless IPM 0-4-0F No. 1

1959 Sentinel four-wheeled shunter No. H001

1960 BR 0-6-0DM No. 03090

1962 Hudswell Clarke ex-Ellington Colliery No.14 0-6-0DM

1979 L&MR 0-4-0 *Sans Pareil* replica

POWERED UNITS

1937 SR 2-BIL motor brake third No. 12123 and driving trailer composite S10656S

1937 SR 4-COR motor open third brake No. S11179S

1959 BR (SR) Class 414 2HAP Unit 4308, motor coach No. 61275 and driving trailer No. 75395

1972 BR Advanced Passenger Train-E set

LOCOMOTIVES AT OTHER LOCATIONS

Barrow Hill Roundhouse, Chesterfield

1902 Midland compound 4-4-0 No. 1000

1905 LNER (GER) 0-6-0 No. 8217

1920 GCR 4-4-0 No. 506 *Butler Henderson*

1958 BR Bo-Bo No. E5001 (Class 71)

Beamish: The Living Museum of the North

1918 Yorkshire Water Authority four-wheel Simplex petrol locomotive No. 1377

1933 Armstrong Whitworth 0-4-0ED D21

1851 Hetton Colliery 0-4-0

Bodmin and Wenford Railway

1874 LSWR 2-4-0WT No. 30587

1899 LSWR 4-4-0 No. 30120

Boness & Kinneil Railway

1960 BR Bo-Bo No. 84001

Bressingham Steam and Gardens

1894 GER 2-4-0 No. 490

1904 GER 0-6-0T No. 87

1909 LTSR 4-4-2T No. 80 *Thundersley*

Colonel Stephens Museum, Tenterden, Kent

1893 S&MR 0-4-2WT No.1 *Gazelle*

Darlington Railway Museum Head of Steam

1825 S&DR 0-4-0 No. 1 *Locomotion*

1845 S&DR 0-6-0 No. 25 *Derwent*

1885 NER 2-4-0 No. 1463

1919 LNER 0-8-0 No. 901

DIDCOT RAILWAY CENTRE

1857 Wantage Tramway 0-4-0WT No. 5 *Shannon*

1985 GWR 4-2-2 broad gauge *Iron Duke* replica

EAST ANGLIAN RAILWAY MUSEUM

1949 BR EMU Class 306 three-car set No. 306017

EAST KENT RAILWAY

1959 BR Class 108 DMU DMCL No.51562 and DMBS No.51922

FREIGHTLINER GROUP LTD

1959 BR Class 09 0-6-0DE No. 09017

GREAT CENTRAL RAILWAY

1912 GCR 2-8-0 No.63601

1925 SR 4-6-0 No. 30777 *Sir Lamiel*

1951 BR 4-6-2 No. 70013 *Oliver Cromwell*

1960 BR Class 33 Bo-Bo D6535

GREAT CENTRAL RAILWAY (NOTTINGHAM)

1972 BR Bo-Bo High Speed Train prototype power car No. 41001

GWILI RAILWAY

1897 TVR 0-6-2T No.28

LEIGHTON BUZZARD NARROW GAUGE RAILWAY

1937 Yorkshire Water Authority four-wheel diesel-mechanical locomotive No. 187105

LONDON TRANSPORT MUSEUM, COVENT GARDEN, LONDON

1890 City & South London Railway electric underground locomotive No. 13

MID HANTS RAILWAY

1926 SR 4-6-0 No. 850 *Lord Nelson*

1934 SR 4-4-0 No. 925 *Cheltenham*

MIDLAND RAILWAY-BUTTERLEY

1866 MR 2-4-0 No.158A (1978-7016)

MILESTONES MUSEUM OF LIVING HISTORY, BASINGSTOKE

1910 Avonside 0-6-0ST No. 1572 *Woolmer*

MUSEUM OF SCIENCE AND INDUSTRY: MANCHESTER

1829 Novelty – replica incorporating parts from the original locomotive.

1873 IOMR Beyer Peacock 0-6-0T Pender sectioned exhibit

1944 Battery Electric

1954 Class 77 EM2 No. 27001 *Ariadne*

1929 South African Railways GL class Garratt No. 2352

1911 Pakistan Railways No. 3157

1992 Planet – replica L&MR Planet class 2-2-0

1951 RSH 0-4-0ST Agecroft No. 3

NORTH NORFOLK RAILWAY

1957&8 BR Class 101 DMU DTCL No.54352 and DMBS No. 51192

RIBBLE STEAM RAILWAY

1865 LNWR 0-4-0ST No. 1439 (1978-7015)

SCIENCE MUSEUM, LONDON

1813 Wylam Colliery 0-4-0 *Puffing Billy*

1829 L&MR 0-2-2 *Rocket* original

1845 LNWR 2-2-2 No. 1868

SCIENCE MUSEUM, WROUGHTON

1845 Tender from LNWR 2-2-2 from Columbine No. 1868

1901 Glasgow Corporation four-wheel tramcar

SOUTH DEVON RAILWAY, BUCKFASTLEIGH MUSEUM

1868 SDR 0-4-0T broad gauge No. 151 *Tiny*

STAINMORE RAILWAY COMPANY, KIRKBY STEPHEN EAST STATION

1875 NER 2-4-0 No. 910

STEAM - MUSEUM OF THE GREAT WESTERN RAILWAY, SWINDON

1897 GWR 0-6-0 No. 2516

1903 GWR 4-4-0 No. 3440 *City of Truro*

1923 GWR 4-6-0 No. 4073 *Caerphilly Castle*

1925 GWR 2-2-2 *North Star* replica

1927 GWR 4-6-0 No. 6000 *King George V*

1947 GWR 0-6-0PT No. 9400

STEPHENSON RAILWAY MUSEUM, NORTH SHIELDS

1904 NER electric motor luggage van No. 3267

STREETLIFE MUSEUM – HULL

1957 Sentinel 0-4-0 steam shunter Works No. 9629 *Frank Galbraith*

VALE OF BERKELEY RAILWAY, SHARPNESS

1924 LMS 0-6-0 No. 44027

WENSLEYDALE RAILWAY

Leyland Motors experimental diesel rail bus LEV1 No.RDB975874

THE JAPANESE BULLET TRAIN THAT JOINED THE NATIONAL COLLECTION

It is neither a steam locomotive, nor is it British. However, one of the 10 most popular exhibits in the National Railway Museum at York is a power car from the Japanese Shinkansen or Bullet Train.

The 82ft-long Series 0 power car, built in 1976 and capable of 125mph, was presented to the museum by West Japan Railways.

The only Shinkansen to be on display outside Japan and the first railway vehicle built and run outside Britain to enter the National Collection is to be found in the Great Hall.

The bullet train arrived in April 2001, finishing its journey from Japan by being towed over part of the East Coast Main Line, a route that it could never physically run over by itself!

To enter the museum, the power car had to be unloaded at York's carriage works and then brought down the ECML in the early hours. While Britain's network has a 4ft 8½in track gauge the same as Japan, the Bullet Train is much wider overall than anything in the UK and does not fit the loading gauge.

Railtrack agreed to shut down the ECML early one Sunday morning and temporarily moved around 30 signals and switchboxes, which would have been in the way, but then replaced them again once the Bullet Train had passed by. Also, special couplings had to be made to join the Japanese vehicle to the locomotive that towed it on its short journey.

The last few yards into the Great Hall

The Shinkansen power car in the Great Hall of the National Railway Museum at York. ROBIN JONES

also proved a challenge. The museum's exhibitions team eased the Shinkansen from the tracks surrounding the museum's turntable, using equipment normally used to rerail derailed stock.

Today's visitors can take a seat inside the Bullet Train and find out what makes it one of the greatest engineering icons of the modern age.

The Bullet Train neatly reflects the international stage of high-speed rail development, and says much about railways across the world in the Sixties.

The Shinkansen commenced operating in 1964, only four years after BR Standard 9F 2-10-0 No. 92220 *Evening Star* was built. It shows how dedicated-track high-speed systems could be successful. The

development of high speed on existing networks within the UK was at that time the only option, so to contrast the Bullet Train programme and the Advanced Passenger Train scheme is a fascinating exercise.

The differences of technology and the loading gauge enable a far more airline-style operation with the Bullet Train, with Britain's HS1 and planned HS2 only now beginning to show how the concept can work in the UK. The NRM's Bullet Train car is the only vehicle outside Japan and was built in 1976, running until 2001.

Today, the power car is a very much valued and appreciated part of the collection.

London, Brighton & South Coast Railway 0-4-2 No. 214 *Gladstone* was the first of the B1 class, the last express passenger design of locomotive superintendent William Stroudley. All of the 36-strong class were named after politicians, but they were collectively referred to as 'Gladstones' after the first. Withdrawals began in April 1910 and the last in service, No. 172, was withdrawn in 1933. The Stephenson Locomotive Society managed to save No. 214 as a static exhibit. *Gladstone* is the only LBSCR tender engine to be preserved, and is now on display in Station Hall at the National Railway Museum in York complete with the regalia with which it was decorated for the Diamond Jubilee of Queen Victoria in 1897. ROBIN JONES

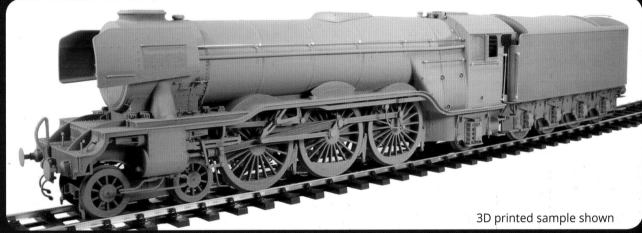

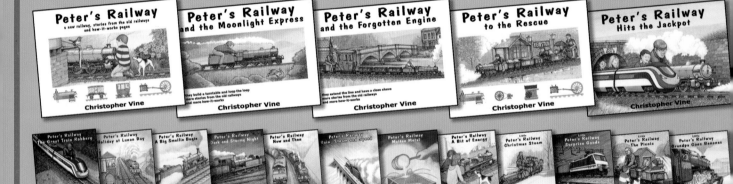

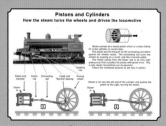